Pearls of
Country Wisdom

Pearls of
Country Wisdom

Hints from a Small Town on
Keeping Garden and Home

Compiled and Edited by Deborah S. Tukua

THE LYONS PRESS

All photographs by Deborah S. Tukua with the following exceptions: page x and page 142 by Ray Stafford; page 149 by Roberta Crude.

Designed by Compset, Inc.

Printed in the United States of America

ISBN 1-58574-105-1

The tips and information in this book are intended to be a help to all who read them. They are not intended for use in place of professional medical advice. We cannot assume any liability of responsibility for any health, food preservation, or other advice given herein. Use at your discretion, please.

Contents

Introduction

A word fitly spoken is like apples of gold in pictures of silver.

Proverbs 25:11

When our family first made the move from suburbia to the country in the summer of 1995, there were many, many things that we had yet to learn. For the past four years or so we've been on a hunt for information, collecting tips. I guess you could say that I'm a bona fide tips collector. It costs nothing, creates no clutter, requires no dusting, washing, or maintenance, and I usually gain a new friend in the process. What other hobby could be so beneficial and rewarding?

We appreciated the willingness and helpfulness of those we came in contact with on our pilgrimage to the simple life. When a neighbor, friend, or new acquaintance gave us a little pearl of country wisdom it was a treasured gift. Now that's something we need to remember and share with others. Another little pearl to add to our enlarging strand. So, we began jotting down tips and tidbits as they drifted our way over the last few years.

And here today, we humbly, helpfully hand them your way in hopes of making your journey through life efficient, skilled, and gratifying as you daily complete the works of the hands. The tips included within this text are meant to be of benefit to this generation, although we realize there are those who prefer to reminisce about the good old days rather than to live them over again. Offered herein are helps for the benefit and enjoyment of those heavily reliant on modern technology as common to this age in which we live as well as to those seeking ways of preserving and maintaining a home and farm with little dependence on modern convenience or the system. It is thus a heritage of this country of past and present methods, yielding quality products that will stand the test of time for generations to come.

As stated, this book would not be possible without the neighborly advice received from many folks. Most of them had no idea their suggestions would be recorded herein. In an effort to keep the generous spirit of giving alive, we share them with you now in this book format. To all those who so graciously shared your pearls of knowledge and wisdom we extend our heartfelt thanks.

A sincere and special word of gratitude goes to the following generous people from whom we have learned much: Marilouise Wilkerson, Coming Home Readership Family, Jeanita Vaughan, Susan Dahlem, Bonnie Plasse, Mike & Ginger McNeil, Jeanne Mange, Chester & Ann Meeks, Tim & Vicki West, Brooks Fuller, Debbie Blazei,

Bonnie Hill, Cliff & Darlene Millsapps, Arlene Nyhof, Bobby Hopkins (Farrier), Teresa Meyers, Mary Wilson, Annette Godwin, Carolyn Hensley (Goat Breeder), Joyce Thomas, Toni Holt, Sandra Curle, SuDawn Peters, Suzan Shearin (Sheep Breeder), Barbara Wilkins, Corinna Fromm, Arlie Pigg, Vicki Benoche (Nurse-Midwife), Ray (Retired Photographer) & Delores Stafford, Tiffany Tukua, Leslie Mullen (Grain Mill Rep.), Lowell & Rita Morgan, Paul Barber (Land Surveyor), Edward Norwood (Land Surveyor), Hugh Godwin, Naomi Yoder, Deloris Massey, Kathryn Horst, Mike & Lisa Hankins, Eli Mast Family, B. E. English (Ginseng Grower), Tom & Jewell Helton, Erik Tukua, Debi Pearl (Midwife, Herbalist), David Tukua, Jim & Robin Brashear, Louise Grass, Cheryl Hanback, T. J., Tom & Kathy Slayman, Meat Department at Daniel's Cee Bee in Collinwood, patrons of Sanitary Barbershop in Waynesboro, and the longriders at Davy Crockett Days in Lawrenceburg, TN.

And most of all, to my beloved husband, Lowell Tukua, who got us here in the first place! Much to my delight! He is my partner, a modern-day pilgrim – pioneer and encourager, never fearful of striving forward. Thus, carrying me along to higher levels and extraordinary endeavors in our journey through life than I would have ever ventured alone.

Cordially,
Deborah Tukua

General Household Tips

The arrival of the mail is a high point in the day. Ours arrives at noon. We don't see the mail carrier coming unless we have a package because our mailbox is one-quarter of a mile from the house. It's such a nice walk to the mailbox though. In the summer, the children and I especially appreciate the coverage from trees on the hillside. The foliage on the towering trees shades our path down the lane like a line of lace parasols held against the sun, allowing only a glimmer of light to shine through now and again. It also gives us a chance to spot any newly born calves in the field and to exchange glances with them, admiring their soft features and adorably big brown eyes. Give me a letter or postcard that I can hold in my hand and read again and again, until I am satisfied. When I get behind in my correspondence, which seems to be too often these days, postcards come to the rescue. I'd rather send a postcard than nothing at all. Of late, I've been designing and making my own postcards in hopes of adding a friendly personal touch in the same way that letters written by hand offer. From my pen in hand to yours I write, no formalities needed here, we're among dear friends!

🦋 *1* 🦋

Save used cooking grease in a jar and store in the refrigerator until you've accumulated enough to make soap.

🦋 *2* 🦋

When rendering (melting down) used cooking fat for making soap, halve a potato or two and place in the pot to absorb the unpleasant odors. After the fat has melted, strain before using.

🦋 *3* 🦋

In soap making, tallow: beef fat, makes a longer-lasting soap. Lard: pig fat, makes a soft bath soap. Coconut oil has a drying effect, but produces lather and olive oil is good for dry skin and to offset the drying effect of coconut oil.

See Cleaning section for more on soap making.

❦ 4 ❦

Don't throw out old window screens. They're perfect for drying herbs on. Lay a second screen on top of the first one containing the herbs to keep them from blowing away.

❦ 5 ❦

Paper sacks also make great herb dryers. Put herb leaves in a paper sack and tie the top or fold it over twice. Don't fill the bag more than half full. Note the contents on the front and store in a dry place such as your pantry, away from direct sunlight. Shake the herb bag daily. Herbs should be completely dry in a week. Remove and store dried herbs in a dry, airtight container. Glass jars with lids work great.

🌿 6 🌿

Save and cut off the front of any greeting cards that you receive. Instantly, you have a free postcard ready to use.

❦ 7 ❦

Recycled greeting card covers can be used to decorate the tops of gift packages. Tape a card cover to the package and trim the borders with ribbon and bow.

❦ 8 ❦

Use left over rolls or remnants of washable wallpaper to line shelves or drawers, to cover cardboard boxes, to wallpaper the inside of a doll house, or to cover a small bench, including the legs!

❦ 9 ❦

Make a linen press for your fine napkins. Glue wallpaper to two squares of illustration board cut slightly larger than your linen napkins. Place the napkins flat in between the covered squares and tie together with large ribbon. Napkins will be neatly stored until needed.

🦋 *10* 🦋

To add extra cushion when shipping fragile items, open out empty egg cartons and line the perimeter of the box.

🦋 *11* 🦋

Use felt, silk, or nylon pantyhose to polish candles to a radiant finish.

❧ *12* ❧

Don't throw away a light bulb that has suddenly gone out until you retighten it or tap lightly on the glass base as it may have become loose. Check your wall plug to make sure it is plugged in securely.

❧ *13* ❧

Especially in the hot summer season, don't open the freezer door several times a day. Instead, determine what you will need for the entire day, and remove those foods from the freezer all at once. Store those foods in the refrigerator or spring box until needed.

🥢 *14* 🥢

During power outages in the cold of winter, refrigerated foods can be chilled in a wooden window box or platform attached to a convenient window on the house.

🥢 *15* 🥢

A heavy wire basket (such as a freezer basket) can be placed in the spring branch to store perishable food items such as milk and will keep them from floating away. For waterproofing, place smaller items such as butter and cheese in a gallon-size glass jar before setting in the spring box.

❧ *16* ❧

To determine if weatherstripping on a door seals out air leaks or needs replacing, light a match or hold a lit candle and move slowly in front of where the door and jamb meet. If the flame flickers, the outside air is entering the house.

❧ *17* ❧

To remove unpleasant odors in the bathroom, strike a match and then blow it out, allowing the smoke to infiltrate the room.

❧ *18* ❧

A compost toilet doesn't require the expense and maintenance of a septic tank. In fact, you can make your own environmentally safe simplified camp version of a compost toilet by using decaying sawdust in a bucket. Place a toilet seat on top and you've got a rustic compost toilet.

🐦 19 🐦

Cover your windows during the heat of day in summer. A large cloth or blinds on the porch further reduces glare, heat, and direct sunlight inside the house.

🐦 20 🐦

If you need to leave entrance steps or a stairway accessible while painting, run a long piece of masking tape down the center of the steps or stairs. Paint one half one day and the other half the following day. Remove the tape before painting the second half.

21

For painting jobs that last a day or two, when taking a break, place the paint brush in a plastic storage bag and store in the refrigerator. This will keep the brush from drying out and you will only have to clean it once when the job is completely done.

22

Free or cheap wrapping paper can be acquired from your local newspaper. Excess newspaper is left on the roll. Ask if it's available. If it's not free, then it is usually sold by the weight left on the roll. The unprinted newspaper can be stenciled and decorated for wrapping paper. Cover your kitchen table with it on a rainy day and let the children draw or paint a huge mural. Newspaper can also be used to cover folding tables for large, informal buffet dinners. Make long banners with personalized messages on it for special occasions.

🐦 23 🐦

Do you have trouble keeping your correspondence current? Keep stamped postcards handy to answer letters faster. When you only have ten minutes, but you really need to write, let postcards come to the rescue.

🐦 24 🐦

Put your postman to work for you. If you need a package mailed from your rural address, no need to drive to the nearest post office. They offer a pickup service. There are certain forms and envelopes available, but our carrier doesn't require them. We just write how we want the package mailed—first class, parcel post, or book rate—and they take care of the rest. No need for exact change, they will leave your change in an envelope in your box the following day. Mail carriers also sell stamps. No need to drive into town for those either.

❧ 25 ❧

Provide a quick and easy way for your correspondence to be answered. Use 2 postcards purchased from the post office. First, address the postcard and write your message on the back as you normally would. Take the second postcard, address it to yourself and staple it to the back of the first. In a corner somewhere on the front of the first postcard, write: "Remove staples for message." The receiver will remove the staples, read the note, and then easily respond, thanks to you.

❧ 26 ❧

When it's time to pack up the dishes for a move, instead of using newspaper and getting ink all over the dishes, place cloth napkins or placemats in between them. Or, you can wrap several plates or platters up in a table cloth.

❧ 27 ❧

Instead of saving coins in your piggy bank, save your dollar bills. They add up quickly.

❧ 28 ❧

New at spinning? Or teaching the children to spin? Practice using the cotton that comes inside bottles of vitamins!

❧ 29 ❧

To prolong the life of film for your camera, refrigerate until ready to use.

❧ *30* ❧

Do you take photographs often? Label the month and year on the outside of each envelope. Number the envelopes in sequence too. On the envelope flap, write the subject matter, event, occasion, etc. to locate later at a quick glance. File the envelopes of photos in a storage container by date. If you remove a photo from an envelope temporarily, write the year and the envelope number on the back, so you can easily return it to the correct envelope in your filing system. When making up albums, you'll also appreciate having the photographs filed in chronological order with general notations.

❧ *31* ❧

Use a slow cooker or crock pot as a very safe way to melt wax when candle making.

⚜ *32* ⚜

Making candles? To strain beeswax, pour melted wax into a pitcher or coffee can. Put a trouser stocking or pantyhose over the top and rubber band it to the can. This acts as a strainer to filter out any particles of debris.

⚜ *33* ⚜

If you have broken candle sticks or part of a candle left after the candle wick has burned down, melt the wax and pour into an oiled ice cube tray until set. Save and repeat the process until you have enough wax to make a chunk candle. To make a chunk candle simply place various colors of cubes of wax into a candle mold with a wick insert. Then, melt clear paraffin wax and pour on top of the wax cubes, filling the mold.

❧ *34* ❧

A neck tie caddy makes a great device for dipping multiple taper candles. Just tie a strand of candle wick onto
each metal rod with a washer tied to the end for weight
and dip the wicks repeatedly into the melted wax.
Voila, multiple taper candles made at once.

❧ *35* ❧

Make fire starters reminiscent of pioneer buffalo chips.
Fill a disk-shaped plastic mold with stubs of straw and

pour hot melted beeswax on top. Allow to cool. When solid, remove. To start a fire, place on newspaper and light.

🕊 36 🕊

Zipper stuck? Rub a candle stub back and forth across the zipper to help it glide smoothly.

🕊 37 🕊

Here's a safe way to shed light. Insert a candle wick into a cork stopper. Float in a mason jar filled with olive oil or even used cooking oil for light. If the jar tips over, the oil will extinguish the flame.

❦ *38* ❦

Save attractive tins and sea shells for candle holders. Place a votive or tea light candle in either and pour hot melted wax until filled.

❦ *39* ❦

Chill candles in the refrigerator several hours before using. Cold candles burn slower and longer.

❦ *40* ❦

Store candles flat, never upright, to prevent warping.

❧ *41* ❧

To make your own waterproof matches, dip just the tips into melted wax. Apply a thin coating and allow to dry on a piece of wax paper. Store in a plastic bag, tin, or other waterproof container.

❧ *42* ❧

Candle wicking can be made at home with household white string or carpenter's chalk line. Soak either of the two in a solution of: 3 T. salt, 6 T. boric acid, and 3 cups water for 12 hours. Allow to dry completely, then braid two or three strands to form the wick.

❧ *43* ❧

To stiffen candle wick, dip in melted paraffin wax.

❧ *44* ❧

Cereal boxes can be used to hold magazines and newsletters. Cut away the top and halfway down one narrow side and your file box is ready. Cover with contact paper, if desired.

❧ *45* ❧

Cut worn cotton socks at the ankle. Use the stretchy top part to absorb moisture from the outside of drinking glasses and to help keep toddlers' and infants' hands from getting too cold when drinking juices from bottle or glass.

46

For convenience, every home needs a tool drawer equipped with tape measure, screwdriver, hammer, pliers, cup hooks, picture hanging wire, nails, and screws in a variety of sizes.

47

To purify water, add a few drops of bleach to a gallon jug of water.

48

A disposable funnel can be easily made by cutting a plastic juice or milk container just below the handle. Turn the top portion upside down and you have a handy funnel with handle!

🐝 *49* 🐝

Lose a pin in the frame of your eyeglasses? For a quick, temporary fix, thread dental floss through the hole and tie a couple of tight knots. Trim away the excess and the dental floss won't be noticeable. It threads easily and is quite sturdy. In fact, you may forget that you need to replace the pin at all.

🐝 *50* 🐝

Need to file a snagged fingernail, but forgot to bring along a file? If in a hotel or restaurant, rub your fingernail back and forth across the grout in between ceramic tile. If outdoors, locate a block of wood, minus the bark, and use as a file.

🐚 *51* 🐚

Find a nice baking pan at a garage sale, but not sure whether it's aluminum or stainless steel? Give it the scratch test. Take a pocket knife and gently scrape along an edge. If it flakes off, it's aluminum.

🐚 *52* 🐚

Many country dwellers use kerosene in their household oil lamps because it is less expensive than lamp oil. Here is a way to neutralize the smell of kerosene when using as lamp oil. Add 3 oz. lime to 1 gallon kerosene, stir, and strain through several layers of cheesecloth or muslin. Add oil-based scent or color, if desired.

❧ *53* ❧

Want to start a fire in the fireplace without the bother of wadding up newspapers and chopping kindling? Mix 5 lbs. sawdust with 1 quart fuel oil (used car oil is ideal, if you change it yourself.). Allow one hour for complete absorption and store in an airtight can. When starting a fire, sprinkle a little around small logs or split a large one, and then light. This mixture is highly flammable!

❧ *54* ❧

Need an old-fashioned chimney sweep? Here's the next best thing. Chimney Soot Remover. Mix 1 cup salt and 1 cup zinc oxide powder. Mix and sprinkle occasionally on a hot fire to keep the flue clean and smoke free. Simple Variation: Throw a handful of salt on a blazing hot fire to clean soot out from the chimney.

🦋 55 🦋

Rats and mice are born to gnaw. If they've started gnawing on a wall or baseboard in your house or outbuildings, use this seal to put a cease to it. Rodents can't chew through this! Combine 1½ cups asphalt, 1¼ cups kerosene, 2 cups powdered cement. Mix with trowel until like putty. Seal holes.

🦋 56 🦋

Chemical-Free Cockroach Exterminator. Combine 4 T. borax, 2 T. flour, and 1 T. cocoa powder. Set out in open containers in kitchen cabinets, behind the refrigerator, etc. away from small children and pets and feed the nasty creatures a final meal.

🦅 *57* 🦅

Ingenious Rat Poison! This remedy usually does not appeal to dogs or cats and is much safer than commercial poison. Mix powdered cement and flour in equal amounts. Set an open container of powder next to a pan of water, yet away from children.

🦅 *58* 🦅

Carpenter Ant Exterminator. Mix 2 quarts kerosene and 2 cups moth crystals until dissolved. Pour into spray bottle and spray in ants' path.

🦅 *59* 🦅

Use egg cartons as a palette to mix and contain different colors of paint for the junior artist.

❧ 60 ❧

Pipe cleaners are easy and fun to use as candles on a birthday cake or in place of candle wicking. They're stiff, stand up well, and burn bright due to the metal core.

❧ 61 ❧

When you live in the country, getting to the library isn't always easy. Establish a home library. This can be relatively easy and inexpensive to do. Call the school board in the nearest big city and inquire about discarded school library books. When we lived in North Florida, a friend and I drove to the Book-Give-Away center and literally filled her van with boxes of books. When our children have a topic to research, we often have a book they can use right at home on our shelves. We grouped them: Geography, Science, Hobbies and Crafts, History, Biography, and Fiction. And the best part of all is that they were absolutely free! We have greatly benefited from having them on hand and have shared many with others!

🦋 62 🦋

Want to take up wood carving? Try soap. It has no grain, thus making it ideal for small carving projects and is an inexpensive hobby for the children.

🦋 63 🦋

Dresser drawers stick? Rub a moist bar of soap across the runners to help them glide easier.

🦋 64 🦋

Want to have a little fun with family and friends around the fireplace? Change the colors of the flames. To make yellow flames, throw a handful of salt on the fire. To make green flames, toss borax on the fire.

Cleaning, Bath, and Laundry Tips

One of the first things we acquired when we moved to rural America was a wringer washer. Wringer washers are as American as the Columbus washboard from Ohio. I suppose that's why many of the "country faire" type restaurants position one on the landing. We knew we had finally arrived in the country when washing clothes outdoors with a wringer washer could be done without anyone doing a double take. I guess I cheat a little, because ours is electric. When laundering clothes in the wringer washer I definitely feel like I've done something afterwards. It requires a committed partner to see the job done. I do my part and the machine does its. There is a certain knack to washing with the wringer. As one sock is drawn through the wringer, I join the next sock to the toe. It's like hooking up boxcars. But the challenge is to do so while the train is moving. I try to keep a continuous line of clothes going through the wringer.

The time I enjoy laundering clothes the most is when it's time to wash the "whites." That's because I can draft a willing partner, our toddler son, to help Mama. As I wring out each sock, briefs, handkerchief, etc. I hand it to Josiah. He carries each item dutifully to the basket or dryer, whichever I ask of him, and hurries back for yet another item. This keeps me from slowing down as he is back from his brief tour of duty for the next assignment before I hardly have time to wring out the next garment for him to carry. I try and have a lot of little items handy to keep him moving, because once he gets started on his mission, he's quite into it. The finale is when he gets to close (or "slam," I should say) the dryer door with a full arm swing and flair that only a little boy could so proudly display.

🐦 65 🐦

To remove the smell of smoke from a room, fill a glass jar with vinegar and place a large oil lamp wick inside the jar. It will absorb the lingering odors.

🐦 66 🐦

To remove spider webs from the hard to reach corners of windows or walls, use a long feather collected from the nearest duck pond or poultry farm. We used one left behind from a neighbor's roaming peacocks. A long turkey feather would do just as well.

🐦 67 🐦

Keep a spray bottle of water and a sponge in the bathroom. To help keep the counter, tank lid, and toilet base dust free in between cleanings, just before guests arrive, moisten the surface with water from the spray bottle and wipe clean with a sponge. With a night light left on and the windows open, it's no wonder that cleaning the counter of bugs seems to be a daily task in the spring and summer months.

🦋 68 🦋

Save water and time. You can do two things at once. Clean the shower stall when you take a shower. Just turn on the shower for a minute before starting. The entire surface is now wet and you're there. No time like the present to get the job done!

🦋 69 🦋

Even young children can sort socks if everyone is assigned one particular sock type or color. Buy multiples of the same sock. Example: One boy's socks can be all gray, Dad's white with a blue band. Another son's socks, white with a gray heel, etc.

✿ *70* ✿

When sons reach a shoe size close to Dad's it's hard to tell their dress socks apart. Give each family member a mesh zipper bag to house their dirty dress socks to avoid separation and confusion in the laundry process.

✿ *71* ✿

Use large safety pins to match sock mates before placing in a dirty clothes hamper.

🦋 72 🦋

Provide several clothes baskets for help in presorting laundry. Place a basket in the bathroom for easy placement of whites after bathing. In the laundry room, locate one basket for jeans and play clothes that are heavily soiled. Designate another basket for delicate or dress clothes. Each person old enough is responsible for properly sorting his or her dirty clothes daily. This gives you a head start on wash day and assists in determining which items are backlogged, needing to be washed first.

🦋 73 🦋

A wringer or James washer is the most economical and environmentally friendly washing machine around. There is usually no need to change the water after each load, so you won't add laundry detergent as often. The water in the rinse tub can be used several times over as well. And in addition, you control the length of time the machine agitates. Start by washing the least dirty items first. Underclothes may only need to be agitated for 3 to 5 minutes. Therefore, you could very well finish washing with a wringer washer sooner than you would with a fully automatic washer. How's that for progress! (If you want to wash only one item by itself, no need to feel wasteful. Just reuse the water on your next load.)

74

Does your family like to work puzzles? Color code each puzzle piece on the backside with a uniform color marker and the child's name it belongs to. Let the children do the color coding as soon as they receive a new puzzle. This will help everyone put things back in the proper place without loss. A great help toward organization.

🦎 *75* 🦎

Need more pant hangers? Take an empty aluminum foil roll and make a cut lengthwise across the bottom. Fit it over a wire clothes hanger and trim the sides to fit if necessary. This will keep the slacks from getting creased on the wire.

🦎 *76* 🦎

Found a really good vintage book at a recent sale? Great find, but it may have a musty scent. Rid the musty odor by sealing the book in a paper bag or plastic storage bag with kitty litter for one week.

77

To remove mineral deposits from a clogged shower or sink faucet, place the shower head in a pot of ½ cup of white vinegar and one quart of water and bring to a boil.

78

Debug the house in winter, totally chemical free! Yes, it's possible. Freeze them out. If you've tried sprays, bombs, and traps only to make you sick or the pesky varmints more determined, try this. Spend a weekend away when the temperatures outside are freezing or just below. Just before leaving, shut down any source of heat, and open all the windows in the house. Roaches and their eggs should all be dead when you return. House plants and pets will need to be provided with other living arrangements during your absence as well.

🐦 *79* 🐦

Like using natural baskets, but get some things snagged on them from time to time? Make a fabric liner for your rattan laundry hamper and baskets that will slip inside and up over and around the top edges, like a huge pillow case. A huge bath sheet or bed sheets would make a durable liner and wash up well. To line the inside of a wide basket, set a large towel or bath sheet, size selected to fit the need, inside the basket. Sew 12" of folded ribbon to the four corners of the towel liner and one to each side and tie at the basket top to secure it in place.

🐦 *80* 🐦

No need to purchase an extra cleanser for the bathroom counter tops and toilet if you have liquid or powdered laundry detergent on hand. A little goes a long way! Use it sparingly.

❦ *81* ❦

Special glass cleaners aren't necessary. For a really simple and thorough cleaning, put white vinegar on a lint-free cloth or paper towel and wipe mirror until clean. Dry the mirror with a dry towel.

❦ *82* ❦

For a homemade solution of furniture polish mix 1 t. lemon oil or the juice from one lemon with 2 cups of olive oil, mineral oil, or vegetable oil.

❦ *83* ❦

Dry baking soda or table salt on a sponge makes an effective scouring powder.

☙ 84 ❧

If you have a septic tank, never use bleach to clean the toilet. The bleach kills the bacteria present in the septic system that are necessary for breaking down the sewage.

☙ 85 ❧

Baking soda freshens the refrigerator. Leave a small box open on the shelf.

☙ 86 ❧

Homemade soap is economical to make and has many household uses.

❧ *87* ❧

Grate 1 cup of bar soap to use as laundry soap. If washing in hot or warm water, add the flakes directly to the water in the washer. If using cold water, dissolve first.

❧ *88* ❧

Homemade soap works to remove stains. Wet a bar of soap and rub directly on stain. Launder as usual. Or, make a paste of 1 tsp. flakes and a little warm water. Then rub into the stain. For tougher stains, use a toothbrush to brush paste into stain and launder as usual.

❧ *89* ❧

Garment presoak can be made by grating ½ cup of homemade bar soap and dissolving it in one gallon warm water. Use a whisk to be sure that the flakes dissolve. Allow water to cool. Add garment and soak 30 minutes to 1 hour. Launder as usual.

❧ *90* ❧

Have we given you enough reasons to try making your own soap yet? Old-fashioned Homemade Soap Recipe. If so, you'll need: 2 quarts of melted lard, lukewarm, 1 quart cold, soft water (rain water or spring water is best), and 1 can Red Devil Lye (12 oz.). To make: Dissolve lye in 1 quart cold water. When both the lye-water and the lard are lukewarm (touch the outside of both bowls to judge temperature), slowly stir lye-water into the melted lard. Be careful not to splash lye on your skin. Continue to stir slowly and constantly until the soap is the consistency of pudding and traces. (Trace means that your spoon leaves a trail across the top as you stir.) At this point, pour the solution into molds. Let set overnight. The next day, cut into bars, but leave in the mold. On the third day, remove the soap from the box and stack like bricks to air dry, leaving space between bars for air circulation. Allow to dry for 2 to 3 weeks before using.

🦚 *91* 🦚

Keep a jug of vinegar handy during soap making, in case lye gets on your hands or arms. Splashing vinegar on the skin will stop it from burning.

🦚 *92* 🦚

No need to purchase a soap mold. Take a shallow cardboard box and line it with a plastic garbage bag cut to size.

❧ *93* ❧

Never use aluminum in soap making. Use plastic, glass, or cast iron, and reserve those items for soap making only.

❧ *94* ❧

Soak neglected paint brushes in hot vinegar to clean and make pliable once again.

❧ *95* ❧

Worn-out toothbrushes are just the thing for scrubbing tile grout, around faucets, leaves of house plants, jewelry, and dirty farm eggs.

❧ 96 ❧

Organize the laundry on the clothesline. Place garments on hangers on the clothesline in the order they will be hung in the closet once dry. All blouses hung together first, short sleeves, then long sleeves. Dresses next. Repeat for the next individual, trying to keep each family member's clothes together on the line. When it's time to remove them, they can be taken directly to his or her closet without having to do additional sorting.

❧ 97 ❧

On windy days, pin a clothespin across the hanger and line to ensure it stays where you put it.

🦅 *98* 🦅

Make your own clothespin holder by fastening a metal pair of oval embroidery hoops in the top of a fabric or small burlap sack or even a plastic shopping bag. Then, slip a wire clothes hanger through it. The hanger will move along the clothesline, and the pins are easy to get to when needed.

🦅 *99* 🦅

Hot water, the electric or gas dryer, and the heat of ironing may "set" stains that can never be removed. The simplest way to remove stains is as soon after they occur as possible. Then launder.

⚞ *100* ⚟

When sorting through clothes for washing, remove pins that might tear clothes, turn pockets inside out, turn down cuffs on pants or rolled up sleeves to get rid of sand, grass, and grit before adding to the washer. Give each item a casual going over for stains that might be set in the hot water. Don't forget to check pockets for sharp objects, such as tools, ink pens, or pocket knives.

⚞ *101* ⚟

Soft water will give better results in washing all fabrics. The lime and magnesium in hard water form curds in combination with ordinary soap. Such curds will retain some of the soil in the wash water and more or less cover the fabric, giving it a gray and unattractive appearance. These curds also tend to weaken the fabric in use.

102

Before washing overalls, trousers, and other "work" type garments, use a little scrub brush or old toothbrush to dislodge dirt, sand, or sawdust from pocket corners.

103

Don't hang laundry outside in freezing weather or in an extremely hot sun. Intense cold tends to break down natural fibers. A scorching sun weakens and fades them.

104

Keep changing your method of folding cloth napkins and tablecloths from time to time to save excessive wear on the folds.

❧ *105* ❧

Always hang slacks or any type of trousers by the legs after washing. The wet weight of the garment will take almost all of the wrinkles out, so little pressing will be needed.

❧ *106* ❧

Mattress covers and pads should be laundered about once a month in warm suds for about ten minutes wrong side out. If possible, dry out-of-doors, pulling edges straight while drying. Shake gently while drying to keep from getting stiff and replace on bed while still fresh from hanging outdoors.

❧ *107* ❧

When hanging a coat or dress on the clothesline on windy days, use two coat hangers hooked in opposite directions, and the wind will not normally blow the garment off.

❧ *108* ❧

Need a convenient way to iron large items such as tablecloths or fabric before sewing? Iron on a well-padded table top. First, cover the table with two blankets and a fitted sheet on top for a large ironing board substitute.

❦ *109* ❦

You won't have to iron twice over parts of clothing if you first iron the sections of the garment that can hang off the board, thus avoiding creases. This being: collars, sleeves, cuffs, and belts. Next, iron the body of the garment, which requires a larger space on which to be stretched out. Be sure to iron absolutely dry as you go along. Damp areas will wrinkle again.

❦ *110* ❦

To prevent gloss on dark cottons, linens, silks, and rayon, iron them on the inside of the garment.

❧ 111 ❧

To conserve energy while ironing, slow but steady strokes are best. It's the heat, not the pressure or weight of the iron that does the job.

❧ 112 ❧

To help little ones keep the towel on the towel rod, drape the towel ¼ of the way over the rod and then pin it at the edge of the back of the towel with clothespins. This keeps the towel from falling off onto the floor when young children give it a pull.

❧ 113 ❧

Do you use the safety pin method for keeping up with socks in the laundry? If so, take it a step further. Put safety pins in a magnetic paper clip container to keep them handy. Place a container in the sock drawer of each person's bedroom, one in the bathroom, and last but not least one in the laundry room. No excuses for not matching socks here!

🏵 *114* 🏵

To bleach linen or muslin, moisten with lemon juice. Then, lay flat outside in direct sunlight.

🏵 *115* 🏵

To cleanse and soften the hands after washing dishes or to remove vegetable stains, rub hands well with lemon juice. It will also remove strong odors such as onions from the hands.

❧ 116 ❧

To remove ink or fruit stains and iron rust, rub the stain well with lemon juice. Cover with salt, and set in the sun. For stubborn stains, repeat this process.

❧ 117 ❧

Never use chlorine bleach on cloth baby diapers. Bleach will cause fabric damage.

❧ 118 ❧

How can one bar of soap be in three or more places at the same time? By making it into Liquid Soap! Ingredients: 1 bar of soap (4 to 6 oz.), 1 T. honey, 1 t. glycerin, water. Directions: 1. Grate one bar of soap in the blender. Soap should appear as small flakes. 2. Add 1 c. boiling water and whip in blender. 3. Add ½ c. of tap water (room temp.) and stir in blender. 4. Add 1 T. honey and 1 t. glycerin and stir in blender. 5. Let cool (approx. 15 min.), then whip again. Mixture should be approximately 2 cups. Add enough cooled water to blender until mixture reaches the 5- to 6-cup mark and whip. 6. Pour mixture into containers for storage and allow to cool without the lids on for at least an hour. Mixture will thicken as it sets up. Shake before using, if needed. Note: Herbs such as calendula, lavender, or fresh pine needles can be steeped in boiling water and strained before adding to the grated soap if desired.

119

Tired of spending all that money on cosmetics? An effective and affordable astringent you can easily mix together is equal parts of witch hazel and water.

❦ *120* ❦

After shampooing, rinse your hair with a tablespoon of vinegar added to a quart of cold water to make your hair shiny.

❦ *121* ❦

Whey is good for your hair as a rinse. Pour over clean, wet hair, working in well, then rinse. It's also good for your hands and nails. Soak hands for 5 minutes in warm whey then pat dry.

❦ *122* ❦

A natural deodorant that is safe and effective is an application of rubbing alcohol and aloe vera gel to the underarms.

See Home Remedies section for additional deodorant tips.

❧ *123* ❧

Here's help for dressing your baby or infant. Put socks over each hand to slip the arms into pajama or shirt sleeves easier. It works!

❧ *124* ❧

It's easy on the back to wash babies and little children while standing. Here's two ways to accomplish that.

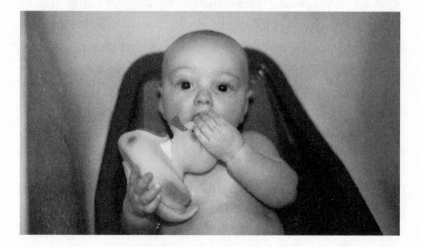

Wash babies in the bathroom sink. Line the bottom of the sink with a towel before adding water to keep the baby from slipping. Roll ¼ of the towel up and place on the edge to serve as a cushion and head support. For young children old enough to sit up, bathe them in a laundry sink tub. It is deep, up off the ground yet holds less water than a bath tub.

🎀 *125* 🎀

Save the mesh sack that your grapefruit comes in. It can be used as a pot scrubber when washing dishes or pots. It does get caught on knives, so don't try using it on sharp items. You can also cut the mesh bag and sew it around a sponge to make your own soft scrubber.

🦋 *126* 🦋

A prewash treatment that works well can be made by saving soap scraps in a jar under the bathroom sink. Add to the jar every time a bar of soap becomes too small to handle. After several additions of soap scraps, sprinkle in a couple of tablespoons of Arm and Hammer Laundry Detergent and cover with very hot water. Once it has cooled, it should be soupy. Stir the mixture together and use an old toothbrush or laundry brush to scrub it into stains and grimy collars just before washing. Keep adding soap slivers, laundry detergent, and hot water to the jar to keep on hand as needed.

🦋 *127* 🦋

Just cleaned your house, but you don't want it to smell sterile when your company arrives? Natural Air

Freshener. Put a pot on the stove three-quarters of the way filled with water and add lemon, apple, or orange peelings, cinnamon, and apple pie spices and simmer. This tip, we've been told, has helped sell houses, too!

❧ 128 ❧

Keep your home smelling fresh while entertaining: keep scented candles or potpourri warmers lit instead of night lights in hallways, the foyer, or bathrooms.

❧ 129 ❧

A natural and beautiful way to add fresh scent to your house is to add fresh-cut fragrant flowers. Place jasmine, magnolia blooms, gardenias, wisteria, roses, honeysuckle, and any other highly aromatic flowers in the entryway, bathroom, guest room, and on the dining table.

❧ *130* ❧

Here's an easy way to add fragrance to every room in the house. *Before* turning on any lights, apply a drop or two of almond, lemon, or vanilla extract to the light bulbs in lamps, ceiling fans, or overhead light fixtures.

❧ *131* ❧

Less is best. The less you have, the less you have to maintain. Your home can be charming without the frivolous, unnecessary knickknacks and collectible items we think we must have. It is much easier to keep a house clean if every shelf, counter, and tabletop is not cluttered with things to dust regularly. If you don't need it, don't bring it home. Consider this before buying something new. Is it necessary or not? Unless it serves a practical purpose, make no purchase.

❧ *132* ❧

Get a head start on tomorrow's laundry. Start one load of whites before bed (if you use an electric, automatic washer). Or, sort laundry into piles, putting the first load in the washer for a quick start in the morning. (This can be done by those of us washing with wringer washers.)

❧ *133* ❧

If you use an electric dryer often, here's an economical way to fight static cling. Pour liquid Downy into a wide-mouth quart jar. Take 1 or 2 high-quality sponges and cut into pieces. Place the pieces into the Downy jar. To use, remove a piece of sponge. Squeeze the excess liquid back into the jar and throw the sponge in the dryer with the wet laundry and dry as usual.

🦋 *134* 🦋

Sorting the garbage is a vital way that we can all be ecology minded. With the proper containers at hand, it really isn't a chore. Here's 4: 1) for wet items and non-burnable kitchen garbage. 2) A pail or bucket with a lid for food scraps to be fed to the animals or compost pile daily. 3) A container near a desk, etc. can hold paper products and burnable items and should be disposed of in the burn barrel as needed. 4) A tub placed just outside for easy access to house glass and aluminum containers for recycling.

🦋 *135* 🦋

Here's a recipe for making your own toothpaste. You'll need to purchase glycerin from a drug store. In a small container measure 10 T. baking soda and 5 to 6 T. glycerin and stir. Add 1 to 2 t. of peppermint flavoring and combine. Spoon out as needed and apply to toothbrush. Give each family member their own little jar.

❦ *136* ❦

Rainwater Laundry Detergent
5 gal. rainwater
1 can lye
7 c. oil, vegetable
1 c. ammonia
2 c. borax
3 c. Wisk
⅛ c. bluing
5-gal. plastic bucket with lid

Pour 2½ gallons of the rainwater into the bucket. Mix lye in slowly with the water and stir with a stick or long wood or plastic spoon. Slowly add the oil while continuing to stir. Add the rest of the ingredients. Stir off and on throughout the first day, as often as possible. Then, stir daily for a week. It will thicken to the consistency of gravy. Measure out for use with a regular laundry scoop.

❧ *137* ❧

Add a little ammonia to dish water to help cut the grease on pots and pans and baking trays.

❧ *138* ❧

Never mix ammonia and bleach when cleaning or laundering.

❧ *139* ❧

Make Laundry Starch. Mix together equal portions of wheat starch and cornstarch. Dissolve 2 t. of this mixture in 1 cup of water. Fill spray bottle with laundry starch.

❧ *140* ☙

Clean lightly soiled wallpaper with a slice of rye bread. The active ingredient is the gluten in rye flour. In fact, commercial wallpaper cleaning solutions often contain rye flour!

❧ *141* ☙

Dishwashing Gel. Here is an easy recipe for making your own dishwashing liquid soap. Grate ½ lb. of bar soap into flakes and place in a large pot with ½ gallon of water. Stir to dissolve flakes. Boil for 10 minutes, stirring frequently. Pour into a glass jar and allow to cool. After the liquid soap has cooled cover to prevent the soap from drying out. As the soap cools, it will thicken to a gel consistency. It is also referred to as jelly soap.

❧ *142* ❧

The best way to remove ladybugs from your windows, carpet, and upholstery is to vacuum them up.

Cooking, Food Preservation, and Kitchen Tips

Canning is probably my favorite method of preserving food. I call it "dinner in a jar" because there's no thawing time as is the case with frozen foods. You can enjoy it right out of the jar or warm and serve. It's a homesteader's "Fast Food in a Jar," convenient and good to eat. Admiring the finished product is as gratifying as its taste. In the summer, I can on the front porch. As I remove the jars from the hot canners, I set them up on the ledge in a straight row. I love it when the whole ledge of the porch is adorned with colorfully filled jars. Then I step back and admire my day's work. It's actually a little saddening to remove the jars and pack them away. So, I make sure that I set a few jars of each food on the shelf of the pantry. Prideful? Maybe so. But well-stocked pantry shelves are something to feel good about. A bounty is a blessing! (Some people call it hoarding food. I call it prudent. The generations before us grew and preserved most of their own food and weren't criticized for doing so. Just because there's a grocery store on every corner doesn't mean we have to be totally dependent on them.)

Look at the variety of foods you've put up for your family. Think of all the wonderful meals you'll share together for months or even a year or two from your efforts. The rainbow of colors of meat, fruits and vegetables, relishes, sauces, and pickles in glass are so pretty. And if you're still not convinced, just ask our laying hens. One summer I lined up a row of freshly canned jars along the edge of the back porch to cool and went inside for a moment. As I walked back toward the screen door, I witnessed a hen pecking her way down the line of jars, hoping to get a taste of the bright yellow squash safely contained behind glass. She didn't miss one. The squash looked as good to her as it did to me, I thought! Only on the farm!

❦ *143* ❦

A wringer washer can also substitute for a pea sheller. Soak the peas in their hulls in hot water before wringing. Place a towel across the top of the wringer to keep the peas from firing back at you and feed them through.

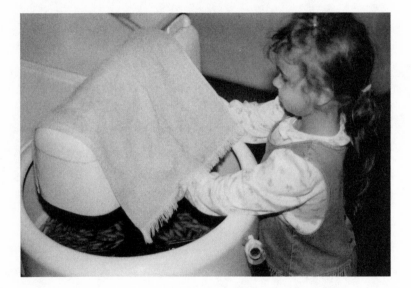

❦ *144* ❦

Use peppermint, dried orange, tangerine, or lemon peels to flavor your tea. Add to water while steeping tea on the stove. Deduct one bag of tea from the pot when adding flavor.

❦ *145* ❦

Start a bread crumb bag. In a plastic bread bag crumble any leftover toast or stale bread. Seal and store in the freezer. Take out as needed. Perfect topping for casserole dishes or when making meatballs or meatloaf. To use as stuffing, place desired amount of bread crumbs in a paper sack, add the seasonings of your choice, and shake to combine.

❧ *146* ❧

Homemade croutons are so delicious that you'll enjoy eating them alone. The secret to delicious croutons is to make from homemade bread! Cut day-old or older bread into cubes. Place in paper bag along with salt and garlic powder. (Experiment with the quantities of spices until you get the blend desired.) Shake to coat cubes and place in a dehydrator or on a tray in a gas oven without turning it on. Or, dry in an electric oven on low heat, about 150° degrees, for approx. one hour or until crunchy.

❧ *147* ❧

Take advantage of the gas stove's drying ability. When the oven is not in use, insert a tray of herb leaves, citrus peels, onion or tomato slices. The low heat emitted from the pilot light will dehydrate your peels. When completely dried, store in airtight containers away from direct sunlight.

❦ *148* ❦

Use your oven as an efficient way to prepare jars for canning. Put clean jars into your oven at the lowest possible setting for thirty minutes. Afterwards, you have hot, sterile jars. (Who said you need a dishwasher to sterilize jars the easy way!)

❦ *149* ❦

Need dinner ready in a hurry? Having jars of home-canned food on your shelves is a healthy way to fast food. Ground or chunks of meat can be packed into pint- or quart-size jars. Add a teaspoon of salt and fill with water. Pressure can meat at 10 lbs. of pressure for 90 minutes. The meat cooks during the canning process. Just pour the meat into a pot or skillet and heat. Ready in minutes.

❧ 150 ❧

Beans are nutritious, but dried beans take so long to cook! Not so when you have jars of home-canned beans on hand. A jar of canned kidney or pinto beans can be used to make chili, bean dip, beans and rice, Spanish rice, Indian tacos, and when mashed with a fork or blender, it becomes an inexpensive version of refried beans.

❧ *151* ❧

Here is the versatile chili bean recipe that is the base to all the good dishes mentioned above.

Canning Chili Beans

10 lbs. of pinto or kidney beans yields 17–18 quart jars

1. Soak 10 lbs. beans overnight in plenty of water. Drain water off.

2. Bring 7 quarts of water to a boil.

3. While water is heating, add these ingredients to a huge pot (water bath canner size):

Ingredients:

4 c. bell pepper, chopped

7 c. onions, chopped

10–20 oz. Worcestershire sauce

¼ c. garlic powder

⅔ c. chili powder

½ c. salt

1½ c. brown sugar

¼ c. dry mustard

Drained pinto beans

6 chili peppers, seeded and chopped (opt.)

4. Add the boiling water to the huge pot and stir through to the bottom to combine. Bring all to a boil.

Allow mixture to boil for 5 minutes on medium-high heat.

5. Immediately fill quart jars, leaving a 1-inch head-space. Run a rubber spatula down the insides of each jar to release any air pockets and to ensure a complete filling. Wipe the tops clean and seal with lids and bands.

6. Process in a pressure canner at 10 lbs. pressure for 65 minutes.

The beans will be fully cooked. To use, just remove from the jar and reheat.

❧ *152* ❧

A 25-pound bag of pinto beans = approx. 50 quart jars of chili beans. Using the ingredients list from the previous recipe, place contents in a large pot. Repeat twice again, filling a total of three large pots. (Each pot should contain the quantity of ingredients noted.) Divide the 25 lbs. of soaked beans in equal amounts into the 3 pots. Add boiling water until full, and stir to blend well. Heat until boiling and fill quart jars.

Process in pressure canners at 10 lbs. pressure for 65 min.

❦ 153 ❦

Yogurt tastes great, but it's pretty expensive, especially when you buy the flavored varieties. Why not make your own? It is easy to prepare. A yogurt machine is *not* required. You *will* need a cooking thermometer.

Making Yogurt at Home
Heat 1 quart of milk on the stove to 180°F. Add 1 t. vanilla and allow milk to cool down to 110°F. Add 6 T. yogurt with live active cultures. (Any store-bought yogurt will do as long as it has the acidophilus. Check the label.) Pour into a clean glass jar. Screw on lid. The jar must be maintained at 110°F. undisturbed for the next six hours, which can be achieved several ways. Select a method from the following: Place in a gas oven without heat. Or, use an electric heating blanket on low. Or, heat water on the stove to 110°F., pour into an

ice chest, set the jar in the chest. Close the lid. It's that simple.

🦅 *154* 🦅

Now that you've got the yogurt, how about a spoonful of homemade granola to eat with it? Here's the recipe: Granola (Yield: 4 quarts) Recipe doubles easily. In a Dutch oven or roasting pan mix: 5 c. rolled oats, ½ c. wheat bran, ½ c. wheat germ, 1 c. chopped almonds, 1 c. sunflower seeds, ½ c. powdered milk, 1 c. coconut flakes. Warm ½ c. vegetable oil, 2 t. vanilla extract, and 1 c. honey, sorghum, or molasses together. Pour over the dry ingredients in the pan and stir through to combine. Bake at 250°F. for one hour, stirring every 10 minutes. Remove from the oven and add 1½ c. dried fruit and stir. Dried fruit suggestions: raisins, apples, papaya, mangoes, pineapples, dates. Enjoy at breakfast with milk or spoon over yogurt or ice cream for dessert. Store in an airtight container.

❦ *155* ❦

Trail Mix Snack is a handy, healthy, and tasty treat to enjoy. To make, take a pint or as much as you wish of the granola noted previously and add ½ c. dried banana chips as well as peanuts or soy nuts and carob chips. You can even add yogurt-covered raisins. A tasty treat made at a fraction of the cost of store brands.

❦ *156* ❦

Turn yogurt into cream cheese? It's easy. Line a colander with a thin cotton dish towel or muslin. Place the colander over a pan or bowl. Pour the yogurt into colander and set it in the refrigerator overnight. When the liquid drips down into the pan, the yogurt will be similar to, but slightly tarter than, cream cheese.

❧ *157* ❧

When making yogurt at home, cow's milk works best. When using goat's milk, add some dry powdered milk to the goat milk to help it thicken. Some people even add a little gelatin to resemble the store-bought versions.

❧ *158* ❧

Measuring out shortening can be quite messy. Use an ice cream scoop. A standard-size scoop holds ¼ cup. Scoop out the shortening and plop into place. No more greasy measuring cup and spatula to clean!

🦋 *159* 🦋

Save leftover food through the week and plan a weekly leftover meal. Save until you have enough servings for your family members. Everyone can have a little of a lot, smorgasbord style. Or each person can have a different entrée. It's a good way to clean out the refrigerator, save on groceries, and give Mom an easy night in the kitchen.

🦋 *160* 🦋

Have soup once a week. Start a soup or vegetable stew starter pot. When you have leftover vegetables, rice, or potatoes put them in the soup pot. Store in the refrigerator. On the desired day of the week, add stock and any other vegetables or grains to your pot, cook, and enjoy. The soup starter blend can be stored in the freezer if a larger accumulation of vegetables is required.

❧ *161* ❧

Ice cube trays are great for storing fresh herbs that tend to lose their flavor when dried. Just place the herb leaves in the trays with water and freeze.

❧ *162* ❧

Add an attractive and flavorful garnish to your next pitcher of iced tea or lemonade. Freeze fresh leaves of mint, lemon balm, or lemon or orange peels in ice cube trays. For the punch bowl, use frozen cubes of any of the above or freeze fresh violets, rose buds, or pansies (all edible) in a clear or light-colored beverage in a Jell-O mold.

❦ *163* ❦

Save those corn cobs. They make a wonderful maple syrup substitute. Tastes great on pancakes and French toast. Directions: Take approx. 2 dozen corn cobs minus the corn, and break in half and again into fourths. Place in a kettle, cover with water, and boil for two hours. Keep the corn cobs covered with water throughout the process. Add hot water as needed. Remove the cobs, strain the liquid. Then, boil down to half. Add one cup of sugar or ½ cup of honey for every cup of liquid left in the pot. Boil down to desired thickness and add a pinch of cream of tartar. Pour into glass jars and seal.

(*Source:* Countryside *magazine*)

🥾 *164* 🥾

Honey-Butter is expensive to purchase, but simple to duplicate at home. Allow one quarter pound of butter to soften slightly at room temperature. Place in mixing bowl and add a little honey. Blend together with a mixer. Add more honey until you have desired thickness. ⅛ t. of cinnamon may be added next as a variation. Pour the spread in glass sample-size jars for gift giving and refrigerate until needed. The perfect companion for warm dinner rolls.

🥾 *165* 🥾

Everyone seems to have someone on their gift list that is difficult to buy for. Homemade gifts show you care. Many wonderful gifts can be crafted in the kitchen. Try making your own gift baskets filled with homemade jellies and jams, muffins, loaves of bread, herbed vinegar, relishes, pickles, cheese balls, or herb teas right off your pantry shelves. Spruce up canning jars with round doilies or calico placed under the band and ribbon.

🦋 *166* 🦋

Here's another gift from the kitchen for the new bride. Select your favorite or special family recipes that people rave over. Take attractive recipe cards and write out the recipes. Place in a recipe file that you have decorated to match and you will be giving a gift that will last a lifetime.

🦋 *167* 🦋

Make your own recipe cards. With pinking shears, cut heart shapes from calico fabric and glue to the corner of index cards. Tie a dozen cards with your favorite recipes with a raffia bow for gift giving.

🐦 *168* 🐦

When bananas get too ripe to eat, place directly into the freezer, peeling and all, to store. Keep adding more bananas until you have enough for your desired recipe. Works great for banana bread recipes. Remove when ready to use, peel, and mash with a fork.

🐦 *169* 🐦

Save time and nutritional value. Leave the peelings on your potatoes, even when making casseroles, potato salad, or mashed potatoes.

🐦 *170* 🐦

Pumpkins were meant to be eaten! Here's how to cook fresh pumpkin. Cut a pumpkin in half and again into fourths if working with a huge pumpkin. Use a spoon to scoop out the seeds and set aside. (The seeds are edible and nutritious too. Roast later.) Place pumpkin skin side down into a roasting pan. Add a little water to cover the bottom of pan and cover. Place 300°F. oven. Pumpkin will take about an hour, unless you are working with a small one. Test center for softness with a knife. When done, it will slice easily. Remove from oven when ready and uncover. Allow to cool slightly to touch. Cut the fleshy part away from the hard outside shell. Chop into 2" to 3" squares. If the pumpkin will be used solely for breads or pies, process the pumpkin cubes in a blender or food processor until smooth. Store in freezer in storage bags or pressure can in pint canning jars.

🦅 *171* 🦅

Baking quick breads in canning jars as a means of preservation was common during WWII. Here's a recipe for Canning Pumpkin Bread:

⅔ c. shortening

2⅔ c. sugar

4 eggs

2 c. pumpkin

⅔ c. water

3⅓ c. flour

½ t. baking powder

2 t. baking soda

1½ t. salt

1 t. cinnamon

1 t. ground cloves

⅔ c. nuts, chopped (opt.)

Cream shortening and sugar. Beat in eggs, pumpkin, and water. Sift flour, baking powder, soda, salt, and spices. Add to pumpkin mixture. Stir in nuts. Pour into clean, greased, wide-mouth pint jars, filling them half full of batter. Bake in jars without lids at 325°F. for about 45 minutes. The bread will rise and pull away from the side of the jars. When done, remove one jar at a time from the oven, clean the sealing edge, and screw lid and band on firmly. Let cool on counter away from drafts. Jar is sealed if lid remains flat when pressed in center. Shelf life is 4 to 6 months if stored in a cool, dry, dark place. If stored in the freezer, it can be kept one year.

🦅 *172* 🦅

Don't discard those apple peelings. They'll make tasty jelly or syrup. A quantity of peelings can be placed in a pot with water and simmered until the skins are soft and the juice from the skins have colored and flavored the water. Make apple jelly with the strained juice or use the apple juice to make mint apple jelly. Apple juice is often the liquid base used to make herb jellies.

🦅 *173* 🦅

Like a healthy, yet tasty substitute for pancake syrup? Honey-Strawberry Spread. Chop ¾ c. strawberries or desired fruit in the blender. Place in a small saucepan with ½ c. clover or wildflower honey. Simmer, stirring frequently, until mixture and flavors are blended. Pour into a small container and store in the refrigerator.

❧ *174* ❧

Pecan meal is about half the price of pecan pieces. Use it instead in baklava and tea rings baked goods.

❧ *175* ❧

When you don't have enough batter to fill up all the muffins cups on a muffin pan, fill the empty recesses half full of water. This will prevent scorching.

❧ *176* ❧

Save time and energy consumption by grating your potatoes and carrots when making soup.

❧ *177* ❧

Do you make cookies, bread, pancakes, or biscuits often? Instead of pulling out the ingredients daily and mixing just one batch at a time, mix several batches at one time minus the liquid ingredients. Put one batch of ingredients into separate Ziplock bags or other airtight containers. Label the contents and store in the refrigerator or freezer. On each bag write the quantities of wet ingredients to be added during final preparation time. (Makes great gifts or bazaar sale items when placed in a cloth bag with bow and recipe card.) Sample recipe follows.

❧ *178* ❧

Instant Cornbread Mix, **Johnny Cake Recipe.** Mix together and place contents in a jar or ziplock bag:
3 cups cornmeal
2 cups wheat flour
6 t. baking powder

½ t. salt
1 cup sugar or ¾ c. honey
½ cup shortening

When ready to bake, add 3 eggs + 2½ cups milk. Stir until moistened. Put in a 9 × 13 pan. Bake at 425°F. for 20 to 30 minutes.

❧ *179* ❧

Keep a box of dried instant potato flakes on hand to thicken sauces and soups. Potato flakes thicken without masking or changing the flavors. The flakes will take on the flavor of the food it is mixed with.

❧ *180* ❧

Whole tomatoes should not be refrigerated.

181

Chopped green tomatoes are a great substitute for chopped bell peppers in casseroles, omelets, etc.

182

Add chopped raw potatoes to over-salted soups while warming. Discard the potatoes, if desired, after they have absorbed the excess salt.

183

Cauliflower steamed with a wedge of lemon will be less bitter.

❦ *184* ❦

When pieces of broken eggshell fall into the bowl of eggs, scoop them out with a larger piece of eggshell. Works like a magnet!

❦ *185* ❦

Here's an easy way to keep honey from sticking to the measuring cup. When measuring honey, syrup, sorghum, or molasses, measure the oil first. Or, rub cooking oil around the insides of the measuring cup.

❦ *186* ❦

Nobody likes pasta that sticks together. Add 1 tablespoon of olive or canola oil to the cooking water.

❧ *187* ❧

To retain the vitamins, don't cut the caps off of strawberries before freezing.

❧ *188* ❧

Don't wash blueberries before freezing. Wash just before eating.

❧ *189* ❧

When preparing jelly or other messy-type sandwiches for young children serve in a plastic sandwich bag. Slide the sandwich up as needed and all the drips will be caught in the bag. Great for preserving clothes during picnics or when serving a host of children.

❧ *190* ❧

Have 1 cup of leftover meat? Get another meal out of it. Take fish, chicken, turkey, or domestic rabbit and chop into small pieces. Add to white cream sauce. Serve over biscuit halves or toast points.

❧ *191* ❧

Poor Man's Lobster. Lightly brush the bottom of an oblong glass ovenware pan with softened butter or olive oil. Place codfish fillets in the pan and brush the top of each fillet with melted butter. Salt and pepper lightly to taste. Bake uncovered until tender at 325°F. When the meat separates easily with a fork, it is done. Small cups of clarified butter should be offered with each individual place setting for dipping the fish, like lobster.

❧ *192* ❧

Make your own soup stock and beef broth. Ask the local butcher for soup bones. If you can, select those with a little meat left on the bone for optimum flavoring. The cost is minimal, but the flavor is maximum. Simmer bones covered with water, vegetables, and desired spices for at least an hour. Strain out and discard vegetables after simmering process. Freezes or cans well.

❧ *193* ❧

No need to peel tomatoes when making spaghetti sauce. Wash tomatoes well, quarter, and chop in the blender.

❧ *194* ☙

Keep sweet potatoes from drying out by oiling the skins with cooking oil before baking.

❧ *195* ☙

Enjoy cottage fries without the grease of frying. Slice potatoes in strips, with the skins on, and season with salt or Cajun seasoning. Lightly oil a cookie sheet and lay the potato strips on it. Place under the broiler until tender. Turn once.

❧ *196* ☙

To get the most juice out of your lemons, oranges, and tangerines place in hot water for several minutes before juicing.

❧ *197* ❧

Gently roll citrus fruit on a table top or in your palm to warm and soften before squeezing to get more juice out.

❧ *198* ❧

Celery tops (leafy part) are tasty too in soups, stews, relishes, and roasts. Dehydrate and store in an airtight container.

❧ *199* ❧

Need a cooling rack large enough to cool a sheet cake? Remove a rack from your oven before heating.

🕸 *200* 🕸

To keep cooling racks from making imprints on cakes, lay a piece of net fabric across the top of the rack.

🕸 *201* 🕸

To keep asparagus from wilting, store upright in a tall drinking glass ⅓ full of cool water.

🕸 *202* 🕸

Don't discard the outer leaves on a head of lettuce. The darker green leaves on the outside contain the most nutrients.

❧ 203 ❧

Iceberg lettuce has little nutritional value. Try mixing all kinds of greens for your next salad—watercress, clover, dandelion, tender beet tops, shredded cabbage, kale, romaine lettuce, and spinach leaves. Many of these salad makings can be gathered from your own garden or found growing wild outdoors in the spring. Much healthier and less expensive when cultivated at home.

❧ 204 ❧

Don't wash fresh farm eggs before storing and you won't need to refrigerate. Water destroys the protective film that keeps out air and odors.

❧ *205* ❧

Eggs should be room temperature before mixing in batters for cooking. If refrigerated, set out 30 minutes before use.

❧ *206* ❧

Before juicing oranges and lemons, grate the rind for use as a flavoring for cookies, pies, cakes, muffins, etc.

❧ *207* ❧

Juices from canned or cooked vegetables and fruits are rich in vitamins and flavor. Don't throw them out! Store them in a glass jar in the refrigerator—one jar for fruit juices and one jar for a vegetable blend. Either can stretch store-bought juice when mixed with it. The fruit juices can also be mixed with baby cereal to add extra nutrients to the baby/toddlers' diet. The vegetable liquids can be used in a soup base.

🦎 *208* 🦎

Cake too dry? Moisten it up before serving. Take thin wooden skewers and randomly poke holes at least ¾ the way through the cake. Pour a fruit syrup across the top and allow it to soak through before serving.

🦎 *209* 🦎

Carob powder may be used as a noncaffeine, healthy substitute for cocoa.

210

Sticky raisins, figs, and dates will come apart easily if placed in your warm oven for a few minutes.

211

It's hard to spread cold icing on a cake. To do so, set the bowl of icing in a larger bowl of hot water and use a warm knife for spreading.

212

It's easy to tint coconut flakes for dessert decoration. Place shredded coconut in a glass jar, not more than half full. Squirt in a few drops of liquid coloring. Cover the jar and shake until color has blended throughout.

❧ *213* ❧

Make fewer trips back and forth from the car on grocery day by carrying groceries in a cardboard box. Leave a box with hand grips (ex: banana box) on either side in your car trunk for grocery day. Sturdier than plastic bags.

❧ *214* ❧

In the hot summer, an ice chest is a handy and practical item to have along, especially when driving at least thirty miles into town. An ice chest keeps orange juice and ice cream fresh on the drive home.

❧ *215* ❧

When planning and preparing meals, remember that eating food the closest to its natural state is the most nutritious. Include plenty of raw fruits and vegetables in your diet daily.

🦢 *216* 🦢

Prevent spoiling of greens and other vegetables in the crisper section of your refrigerator. Line the compartment with paper towels or print-free newspaper to absorb the excess moisture.

🦢 *217* 🦢

To reduce the amount of fat in soups, chicken and dumplings, or roast and gravy, etc., prepare ahead and chill in the refrigerator. The fat will rise to the top and harden. Simply spoon off and reheat.

🦅 *218* 🦅

Make your own cornmeal, inexpensively. Buy bulk bags of regular unpopped popcorn kernels and grind it!

🦅 *219* 🦅

Can your own milk. No need to buy powdered or canned milk for use in cooking and baking when you have a dairy goat or milk cow. Just place the milk in pint or quart canning jars with lids and rings and pressure can at 10 lbs. pressure for 20 minutes. Stock up extra jars to have during dry times!

🦅 *220* 🦅

Use rendered chicken fat for making biscuits or dumplings to serve with chicken dishes. It reduces the need for purchasing shortening and adds a delicious flavor.

221

Zest up homemade pizza dough. Add dried, crumbled bits of tomato and ¼ t. each of oregano and basil to pizza dough before kneading.

222

Add a gourmet flair to your next B.L.T. sandwiches by adding crumbled bits of fried bacon and dried tomato pieces (oregano and basil, opt.) to your next batch of basic sandwich bread dough and knead.

🦅 223 🦅

If you don't have buttermilk on hand, add 2 T. of lemon juice or vinegar to 1 cup of sweet milk and stir.

🦅 224 🦅

To determine whether an egg is fresh, place in a glass of water. A fresh egg will sink in water.

🦅 225 🦅

When purchasing bacon, you get more for your money by buying it in ends and pieces.

🐉 226 🐉

When baking chocolate cakes, dust greased cake pans with cocoa or carob powder instead of flour.

🐉 227 🐉

To keep brown sugar soft, refrigerate in a glass jar or plastic bag with a piece of bread or apple.

🐉 228 🐉

To soften hardened brown sugar, place the amount needed in a pan in the oven at 300°F. for 15 minutes, then proceed with recipe.

❦ *229* ❦

To prevent steaks or chops from curling when broiling or frying, score the edges of fat with a knife every one to two inches.

❦ *230* ❦

Oops! Cracked an egg you were about to boil? It can still be boiled. Just add a teaspoon of salt to boiling water, then add the egg. The contents will not ooze out. The salt will cause the egg white to set more quickly.

❦ *231* ❦

Want to melt chocolate without a messy pot to clean later? Here's how. Wrap chocolate squares in foil and melt in a double boiler. Once melted, carefully spoon out the chocolate.

❧ 232 ❧

To successfully cut a square or rectangular cake, slice a quarter section at a time. This should keep it from collapsing.

❧ 233 ❧

To easily slice cheesecakes and frosted cakes, dip the knife in hot water and dry off to prevent the frosting and cake crumbs from sticking to the knife.

❧ 234 ❧

Brewer's yeast and nutritional yeast are *not* substitutes for baker's yeast. They are nutritional supplements. Nutritional yeast tastes great when sprinkled on popcorn.

❧ *235* ☙

Simple Beginner's Cheese (Queso Blanco). Place 1 gallon of milk in a stainless steel stock pot. Heat to 190° F, stirring occasionally. Remove from heat. Add ½ c. of vinegar or lemon juice and stir. Let rest for 10 minutes as curds form. Pour contents into a colander or strainer lined with cheese cloth or muslin bag. Tie the bag or cloth and hang for one hour, allowing the whey to drain. Salt to taste and refrigerate or freeze. Variation: To make hard cheese, immediately after pouring into colander, season with salt and place cheese in cloth in a cheese press for a couple of hours with 10 pounds of pressure.

❧ *236* ☙

For a really pretty presentation, bake your next pumpkin or banana bread recipe in small, greased coffee cans. It slices into very attractive round cakes.

🦋 237 🦋

Slices of banana bread make great gourmet French toast!

🦋 238 🦋

Cooking healthy foods like dried beans and brown rice takes time. There's a way to fix both nutritious foods without hours of preparation time. Invest in a stainless steel pressure cooker. You can have the same results in *less* than half the time.

🦋 239 🦋

Place flour in a salt shaker and shake when needed or use a powder puff to neatly dust bread boards and other pastry working surfaces.

❦ *240* ❦

To remove excess air from plastic storage bags of food for the freezer, place a drinking straw in the corner and close the bag up to the straw. Draw in a deep breath to remove the air. Quickly pull out the straw and seal the bag.

❦ *241* ❦

A nontoxic substance to ward pests away from your pantry is diatomaceous earth. Spread a thin trail of it around bags and boxes of food, on shelves and the doorway where insects crawl near your food supply. The scratchy surface of diatomaceous earth will deter crawling insects as the sharp fragments of seashells actually cut through the bugs that crawl across it.

242

Buttermilk can be used as a starter in cheese making.

243

Include fresh sprouts in your diet. They are easy to grow at home and are highly nutritious. (See the gardening section for details.)

244

Wheat grass is said to be one of the most highly nutritious foods on this planet. It too is easy to grow at home and juice. (See the gardening section for growing details.)

245

Leftovers are easier to identify in the refrigerator when stored in glass jars.

246

Save empty glass containers such as pickle and mayonnaise jars for storage of dried herbs, rice, beans, and refrigerated foods.

247

Empty mayonnaise jars can be used for water bath canning.

🕊 *248* 🕊

The plastic scoop that comes in boxes of laundry detergent makes a handy rice, flour, grain, or sugar scoop in the kitchen. Leave one in each canister or container.

🕊 *249* 🕊

To keep your iron skillets from rusting, apply a thin coating of shortening or vegetable oil on the inside surface after washing. Never stack skillets damp. After washing, set on a warm stove top for quick drying. Then oil and put away.

🕊 *250* 🕊

Cooking Substitutions
Vinegar = lemon juice
1 T. cornstarch = 2 T. flour

1 whole egg = 2 egg yolks

1 T. fresh herb = 1 t. dried herb

1 t. dried mustard = 1 T. prepared mustard

1 clove garlic = ⅛ t. garlic powder

1 small onion = 1 T. dried minced onion

¼ t. cream of tartar = 1 t. lemon juice

❦ *251* ❦

Culinary Spices Companion Chart

BEEF: Bay leaves, chives, hot peppers, marjoram, oregano, rosemary, peppercorns, savory, thyme

BREADS: Anise, caraway, coriander, dill, marjoram, oregano, rosemary, thyme

PORK: Coriander, nutmeg, cumin, garlic, ginger, hot peppers, sage, thyme

LAMB: Garlic, marjoram, oregano, tarragon, mint, parsley, oregano

VEGETABLES: Basil, chives, dill, tarragon, marjoram, mint, parsley, oregano

❦ 252 ❦

Recipe calls for nut halves or pieces? To economize use peanuts or sunflower seeds.

❦ 253 ❦

Make every step count twice when cooking. When browning fresh ground meat, fry enough for at least two meals. Use the portion needed for that meal and refrigerate extra to use within the week or freeze. Follow the same suggestion when boiling chicken or baking a ham. Prepare more than just one meal's quantity at a time. Make one meat loaf and freeze another. Or, shape meatballs and bake them in the oven. Can or freeze extra for future convenience.

🎋 *254* 🎋

Love the taste of homemade pie crust, but not the cleanup afterwards? Make the crust in the pie pan to be used. Here's how. One Pan Pie Pastry—Yield: 9" pie shell. 1 c. whole sheet pastry flour, ¼ t. salt, ¼ c. oil, and 3 T. water. Place the flour and salt in the pie pan to be used. Measure the oil in measuring cup and add the water. Beat with fork until oil is emulsified. Pour over flour, stirring with fork to distribute moisture evenly. Mix until well blended. Press into shape against pan with fingertips. Bake at 375°F. for 20 minutes.

❧ 255 ☙

Ever have homemade butter start to sour before it's all gone? Don't throw it out. Mix powdered garlic and salt with slightly soured butter for a delicious garlic toast spread!

❧ 256 ☙

Buttermilk adds splendid flavor to corn bread and makes homemade bread more tender.

❧ 257 ☙

Biscuit dough makes the tastiest pie shell and top crust when preparing chicken pot pie.

🦋 *258* 🦋

Hard aged cheeses are best made in spring and late autumn when it is cooler, thus avoiding mold formation on the cheese surface.

🦋 *259* 🦋

Never use an aluminum pot when making cheese or soap. Reserve aluminum cookware for candle making.

🦋 *260* 🦋

Frozen yogurt is easy to make. Simply take yogurt, (homemade or purchased) and add desired fruit. 1 cup of chopped fruit per every quart of yogurt and stir to combine. Sweeten if desired and freeze. That's it!

🐀 *261* 🐀

If you're blessed with a lemon tree, then you'll want to preserve some of that fresh lemon juice to have year-round. Juice your lemons and pour into ice cube trays. (Don't forget to dry the peels for baking later too.) Once frozen, remove from trays and store in a freezer bag. Each cube will yield about 2 T. of lemon juice. Remove as needed for cooking.

🐀 *262* 🐀

It takes about 7 or 8 egg whites to make one cup.

🐀 *263* 🐀

Corn oil keeps longer at room temperature than any other vegetable oil.

❧ 264 ❧

Dampen the rim of a bowl or jar and the plastic wrap will cling better.

❧ 265 ❧

To save on cling wraps, cover bowls with elasticized shower caps.

❧ 266 ❧

Do you have an abundance of eggs? Break each egg open one at a time. Inspect for freshness, then beat lightly. Place one egg into each compartment of an ice tray that has been oiled. Freeze. Once frozen, store in ziplock bags. Remove as many as recipe demands. Allow to thaw before use in baking.

❧ 267 ❧

Eggs can be kept in the freezer up to one year.
See the Animal Section for storing fresh whole farm eggs without refrigeration for up to one year.

❧ 268 ❧

Fresh ground flour contains over thirty nutrients! After milling, nutrients begin to oxidize and within about 72 hours 90% of over thirty nutrients are gone. "Enriched bread" from the grocery store shelves usually replace only 4 of the vitamins to the bread flour! Fresh is best!

❧ 269 ❧

Vitamin C helps sustain the leavening of bread during baking. It also promotes yeast growth causing your yeast to work longer and faster and helps produce acidic atmosphere in which yeast grows best. To liquids, add ¼ tsp. vitamin C powder or a 250 mg. tablet, crushed, per 4 loaf bread recipe.

❧ 270 ❧

Mashed potatoes is a good source of yeast food and natural vitamin C. It acts as a dough enhancer and adds moisture to bread. Makes a lighter, better textured bread.

❧ *271* ❧

Grain to Flour or Flakes Measurements

⅔ c. grain = 1 c. flour.
1 c. oat groats = 2 c. flakes.
3 c. flour = 1 lb. flour, approx.
1 c. rye berries = 2 c. flakes.
2½ c. whole corn = 1 lb. corn = 4¼ c. ground cornmeal.
2¼ c. wheat berries = 1 lb. wheat = approx. 3¾ c. flour.

A 6-gallon bucket of wheat berries will yield approx. 158 cups of ground flour.

❧ *272* ❧

We've all heard how eating oatmeal is good for keeping our cholesterol down. Here are delicious ways to up our intake of oatmeal. Flaking your own oat groats into oatmeal for pancake mix, granola, or Muesli, cobbler toppings, cookies, or meat loaf extenders is a nutritious and inexpensive way to provide meals for your family. The product far exceeds the quality of oatmeal on the supermarket shelves. There are many hand and electric flaking devices on the market, so flake your own! It's easy to do even with a hand meal.

❦ 273 ❦

Muesli is a delicious breakfast cereal. Here's my recipe: Mix the following into a resealable container and store in the refrigerator:

4 c. flaked oats
2 c. dried fruit medley
1 c. coconut flakes
1 c. almond or pecan meal
2 large apples, grated
2 c. milk
½ c. honey

Stir to combine and chill before serving. Spoon portion into a bowl and serve with additional milk and honey, if desired. Use within one week. Note: To store cereal in the pantry, omit the fresh apples and add milk just before serving.

❧ *274* ❧

Canning pickled eggs is a good way to preserve an abundance of eggs. Here's how: Bring 3 c. water to boil. Stir in 3 c. white vinegar and 6 T. canning salt. Add a sprig of dill to each canning jar. Fill canning jars with peeled, hard-boiled eggs. A quart jar will hold about a dozen eggs. Pour in pickling solution and seal. Water bath can in boiling water for 20 minutes.

❧ 275 ❧

Don't confuse your serving pieces of flatware when taking them to a friend's home or group dinner. Paint your last initial on the handle back with fingernail polish.

❧ 276 ❧

Can butter?!! Here's how. Heat glass canning jars (pint or ½ pint size) in a 250°F. oven for 20 minutes (without lids or rings). While jars are heating, melt butter in a deep sauce pan (do not fill over halfway) slowly until it reaches a boil. Reduce heat to simmer and cover. Simmer for 5 minutes. (Watch carefully, if the pot boils over, you'll have a fire!) Pour melted butter into hot jars through a canning funnel. Do not fill the jars more than ¾ full to allow for slight expansion as the butter cools and returns to solid. Wipe the jar rims with a clean damp cloth and seal with lids and rings. They should seal as they cool. After the jars have cooled, put in the refrigerator until the butter hardens. Once hardened, remove from refrigerator, remove the ring and test the lid for a right seal. Stores on your pantry shelf.

🦅 277 🦅

To flavor a pot of beans without adding salt pork, season with kelp instead.

🦅 278 🦅

Wonder why the old-timers never contracted Salmonella? After using a cutting board, it was thoroughly cleaned and heavily salted.

☙ 279 ❧

Here's how a retired meat cutter from Minnesota protected cutting boards from forming bacteria. First, clean the board well. Then, apply a little bleach water solution and rinse. Dry completely. Melt paraffin in an old double boiler. Pour enough paraffin over the board to cover it thoroughly. Take a hot iron (old electric or sad iron) and iron the wax into the board. The melted wax and iron process seals any cracks or open pores in the wood. (This procedure should be repeated periodically as the wax wears away.)

☙ 280 ❧

Too many cooks in the kitchen to remember which towel is for drying hands and which one is for drying dishes? Here's a solution. Embroider or cross stitch the word "hand" on the kitchen towels you designate for drying hands. On the towels to be used for drying wet dishes, glasses, and cookware, embroider the word "dish." When extra help is in the kitchen, there'll be no confusion as to which towel to use.

❧ *281* ❧

Put up sausage patties or bulk sausage. Here's how: Make sausage into patties and lay on trays in the oven and bake. Once brown, place into wide-mouth canning jars. Add 1 t. salt and about ½ cup of sausage drippings to each jar and seal with lids and rings. Pressure can at 10 lbs. pressure for 90 minutes. To can bulk sausage: Place 1 to 1½ pounds of uncooked bulk sausage into each quart canning jar along with 1 t. salt. Add about ½ cup water to each jar and pressure can at 10 lbs. pressure for 90 minutes. (To use, drain water from the jar and drain further on paper towels, then fry in skillet until brown. Bulk sausage is great for use in omelets, pizza topping, casseroles, etc.)

🦟 282 🦟

Storing Butter in Salt Water Brine. Fill a sterilized gallon jug container of glass, stoneware, or plastic ¾ full of fresh cool water. Add a cup of canning salt or other plain salt (without iodine) and dissolve. Place an uncooked egg into the container to test the brine. If the egg floats, the brine is salty enough to preserve butter. If it does not, remove the egg, add more salt, and dissolve. Continue testing until the egg floats. Remove the egg. Add fresh butter and lid. Store the Butter Brine in a cellar, basement, or unheated room. Remove butter as needed.

🦟 283 🦟

Make a healthy soft butter spread at home! Here's a spread that reduces the fat and stretches the butter. Mix equal portions of butter and canola oil together until equally blended. Store the creamy spread in a tub in the refrigerator.

Wardrobe and Sewing Suggestions

A homemade gift shows you care enough to make it from the heart. If you're like me, you probably have a little box that your mother saved filled with special things that you made with your own two hands and a little help. As children, this is the start, where we not only gain skill and know-how, but confidence in our ability to take on new challenges, to try working different things with our hands. After my maternal grandmother passed away, I was given her sewing basket. It has remained as she left it over these past eleven years until recently. Just this summer, my mother bought a beautiful two-tone set of baskets in graduated sizes that have now become my new sewing baskets. Carefully and thoughtfully I transferred the contents of Grannie's basket over into its new home, my new trio of baskets. Yet, I would never consider parting with her pink round sewing basket of many years. Instead, I will again fill it with treasures of sewing, mending, and crafting needs to prepare it for the journey into the next generation, into my daughter's heart and hands!

Believe it or not, the wringer washer helped me through a character weakness. As I mentally prepared for the upcoming transition our family was about to make, moving from "City Kitty" to "Country Cat," my wardrobe had to change too! Practicality became a high priority. As I evaluated whether my dress was selected foremost on the basis of appearance or for practical purposes, the wringer washer had its say. Were there certain clothes that I absolutely would not put through the wringer?!! If so, why not? AH-HA!! It caught me by my costly array and my vanity! Yep. I was still a little too fancy for the country life. Although I had scrutinized the contents of my clothes closet before we moved, I obviously had further weeding to perform. This handy device helped me further my journey into a more simple, practical lifestyle without pointing a finger or uttering a word.

❧ *284* ❧

Save those fabric scraps. For the quilter in the home: Start 3 bins of fabric scraps. On the outside of one write 1", 2nd–2", and the 3rd–3". When you are cutting fabric while sewing, immediately cut up all the remnants into 1", 2", or 3" strips. Strips work great for strip quilting or appliques and craft projects. Sort into the designated storage bin to prepare for your next quilt or braided rug project.

❧ *285* ❧

Fabric scraps make homey and charming crazy quilts, table runners, and matching place mats. Crazy quilts put to good use odd-shaped fabric scraps. Cut your remnants into various shapes and serge around the outside of each piece. With a blanket as backing, lay the remnants in an appealing manner. Pin several pieces into place, overlapping edges to cover the backing. To attach to backing, hand embroider desired stitching pattern around the edges. Continue to pin pieces of serged fabric and embroider into place until the entire blanket is covered. Finish the edges with seam binding and you have a crazy quilt.

🦋 *286* 🦋

Burping Bibs for baby can be made from one piece of flannel sewn to one piece of towel. When using an extra thick towel, no flannel is needed. Cut pieces in an hourglass shape. Pin flannel to towel and serge the edges.

🦋 *287* 🦋

Make a clutch bag out of a quilted place mat. Fold up like an envelope and sew the sides down. Add a ribbon for shoulder strap if desired and closure. Great gift idea.

🦅 288 🦅

Move often? Make curtains with extra long hems so they can be moved from room to room or house to house.

🦅 289 🦅

Make a coat to last your growing child three years! Start with raglan sleeves, making them extra long and use an inner complementary fabric for a pretty cuff that can be rolled down shorter and shorter as the child grows taller. The coat should be made close to knee length or longer, ending up at hip length.

🦅 290 🦅

Pick curtain fabric for the bedroom and kitchen that can be later used to make pretty little girl's dresses or pinafores when a change is desired.

❧ *291* ❧

To get longer usage of a skirt or dress for your growing girls, make a cotton half slip with a prairie-style ruffle or wide eyelet along the bottom at the desired dress length. The eyelet will show as the dress gets too short, giving the dress a longer appearance.

❧ *292* ❧

For growing girls, sew a 2- or 3-inch strip of fabric onto the bottom of skirts and dresses in the same way as when using hem tape. When it's time to lower the hem line, turn down the strip already in place. It will look like the band was part of the design. Oftentimes when letting out a generous hem, we end up with a deep crease that won't wash out, thus causing the dress to appear worn. Turning down the strip at the seam should avoid an unsightly crease.

❧ 293 ❧

Recycle jumper dresses. Turn a too short jumper dress into an apron. Open both side seams and finish 4 raw edges. Leave the shoulder seams in tack. Sew two 3" pieces of ribbon to either side at the waist. Tie into bows. (To make stiff bows guaranteed not to untie, see tip 349.)

Variation: Making a New Apron from a Jumper Pattern (See photo on page 149.)

Cut 2 front and 2 back pieces of the top of an apron pattern and sew together as directed.

Cut four 3" inch strips the width of the fabric (36" or 45") for the waist band/ties of the apron. Sew two pieces together, wrong sides, leaving a 1" opening, turn right sides out and close opening.

Cut two pieces for the skirt of the apron the width of the fabric at desired length. Open the fabric. Gather it at the top and sew to the band. Then sew skirt to bodice. Hem the sides unless the selvage is smooth.

🦋 *294* 🦋

When boxing wool sweaters after winter, cut a circle of fine netting. Fill the center with cedar shavings and tie together with ribbon. This should save the sweaters from moth damage.

🐝 295 🐝

If you have wool jackets or sweaters in your closet, line your walls with thin cedar lumber. If this isn't feasible, take a 1-inch-thick block of cedar. Drill a hole ½-inch down from the top. Insert twine or a ribbon through the hole and tie to the clothes rod right next to your wool garments. Be creative and cut cedar lumber into circles or other shapes for gifts, personal use, or fund-raisers.

🐝 296 🐝

Make sachets filled with cedar shavings and place in dresser drawers to protect wool scarves, mittens, and sweaters from moth damage.

❧ 297 ❧

When storing children's clothes for later use, sort by size and mark the gender, size, or child's age on the outside of the storage container for easy retrieval when needed.

❧ 298 ❧

When using a pattern with multiple sizes, no need to cut off all the smaller sizes. Clip the corners to fold back easily and tape to reinforce. Fold the pattern back to size required.

❧ 299 ❧

Organize and file your patterns. Sort in broad categories. Ex: infant sizes, craft and household patterns, men's items, children's, ladies', etc. This can be accomplished in a cardboard box or in a file cabinet drawer. Use a large sturdy card in between categories, noting the division on the card for ease in locating.

300

Pressing each pattern piece before replacing it in the envelope greatly reduces the space needed to store used patterns. Press so the letter of the pattern piece is centered on the front to reduce time locating specific pieces later. Iron on low setting with *no* steam.

301

When cutting out a pattern for the first time, use a clothespin to keep the pattern pieces together that will be used. All others can go directly back to the envelope after pressing.

❧ *302* ❧

A plastic shower curtain makes an ideal inner liner when making your own diaper changing pad. Cut two pieces of towel or terry cloth, one piece of low-loft batting and a plastic shower curtain cut to desired size. Sew the shower curtain to one piece of towel. Sew the batting to the other. Lay both pieces together, towel sides touching. Sew together leaving about a 6" opening to turn and stitch closed.

❧ *303* ❧

For a diaper changing pad to take along in your diaper bag, sew one piece of a plastic shower curtain to one hand towel.

❧ *304* ❧

Make your own absorbent, high-quality diapers from flannel or receiving blankets.

❧ *305* ❧

Plastic shower curtains make great backing for picnic blankets and outdoor tablecloths.

❧ *306* ❧

Make full or half slips out of flannel for warm winter wear.

✻ *307* ✻

Flannel bloomers offer an added layer of warmth under dresses.

✻ *308* ✻

Wear leg warmers on top of socks or tights for winter warmth.

✻ *309* ✻

Discarded men's neck ties make snazzy piece quilts and other craft projects.

❧ *310* ❧

A quick copy of a bloomer can be achieved by cutting off a pair of thermal or sweat pants. Hem slightly below the knee and encase with elastic to keep from sliding.

❧ *311* ❧

When sewing a shirt or dress, etc. from a particular pattern, make two garments at a time. It takes just a little longer to repeat each step twice as you go along, but you'll have two new garments in not much time.

❧ *312* ❧

Here's a new dress in a hurry! Sew a ready-made, button-down blouse to a gathered skirt. Use a half slip or petticoat pattern for the skirt portion of the dress. Cut the blouse down to just below the waistline. Gather the top of the skirt to fit the shirt at the waistline and sew together. Leave the dress a little loose at the waist to slip over the head. Make a tie belt from the excess fabric you cut from the blouse.

❧ *313* ❧

Before discarding old, worn pants, shirts, etc. remove the buttons, zippers, hooks, and eye closures, etc. Store in designated containers.

❧ *314* ❧

Run out of envelopes? Sew your own! Using an 8½" × 11" sheet of paper, fold up 4" from the bottom. Sew a loose stitch on the machine down both sides in desired color thread. This will leave about a 3" flap at the top to turn down and seal with a sticker or glue stick. To complement the envelope, take another sheet of the same paper and stitch a border using the same thread around the paper for a truly unique stationery ensemble!

❧ *315* ❧

Use a rotary cutter for quick cutting. Cut multiple pieces at a time when crafting or quilting.

❧ *316* ❧

Dread making buttonholes? Try snaps instead. There are snaps made to look just like buttons on the market today.

❧ *317* ❧

Would you like to find someone to cut quilting squares for you without charge? I did. Locate out-of-date fabric swatch books from thrift stores or local interior design firms. All the swatches in a book generally coordinate and are cut to the same size. Just remove the fabric swatches from the book. Peel off the paper labels from the backside and start sewing.

❧ *318* ❧

Life's cooler and more comfortable in cotton. Nylon underpants are hot and sticky to wear. Wear 100% cotton underclothes and garments to keep comfortable in summer. Also 100% cotton sheets are available for a restful night's sleep.

❧ *319* ❧

A retired curtain rod makes a handy shoe rack. Just tack the rod on the closet door, or mount it on the back wall close to the floor so that it projects forward an inch or more and hang shoes by their heels.

❧ *320* ❧

Use old blankets to add a warm lining to a new duvet.

❧ *321* ❧

Save old pantyhose and trouser socks for stuffing throw pillows.

❧ *322* ❧

When towels become frayed on the edges, serge the borders to renew their appearance and life.

🐦 *323* 🐦

Duplicate those expensive hunting shirts. Make or purchase a standard flannel or corduroy shirt. Cover a shoulder pad in coordinating fabric. Serge or zigzag edges of the pad, then sew it to the front shoulder of the shirt where the butt of the rifle will rest. Sew patches from the same fabric on to the elbows and your sportsman will have a handsome hunting shirt.

🐦 *324* 🐦

Duvets are especially handy for young children unable to make their bed. The duvet serves as a sheet, blanket, and bedspread all in one. Duvet directions: Measure your comforter or blanket and add 2 inches to each side. Trim two flat sheets to match these measurements, if needed. With right sides facing, sew the top edge and the two side edges of the sheets together, allowing for a ⅝" seam. Turn under the bottom edge and hem. Sew snaps or buttons and buttonholes to the opening. Turn the duvet cover right side out and insert the comforter. Fasten snaps or buttons and you have a warm and practical bed covering.

🦋 325 🦋

The country look can be had by sewing old quilt tops to bib-type overall tops. Next time the knees of brother or Dad's overalls are too worn to patch, cut off the bib top and transform with a quilted skirt bottom.

🦋 326 🦋

The warmest coats are made of natural materials. Select one with goose down lining or a natural fur such as rabbit when plenty of warmth is needed. Polar bear fur is the warmest of all, which would be needed if and when a trip to the North Pole lies in the future.

❧ 327 ❧

Time is precious. When selecting clothing patterns, look for ones that are uncomplicated to sew. Leave off the extra unnecessary touches that take up hours of time. Stay with the basics, especially if you sew for the whole family.

❧ 328 ❧

Browse the sale tables in the fabric department first. Buy fabrics when they are on sale even if you don't intend to use them until later. Buy corduroy and heavy fabrics at the end of winter when they are on sale for next autumn's sewing session. Buy summer fabrics at the end of the season when prices are marked down.

❧ 329 ❧

Buy children's clothing when on sale, even those a size or two larger and place in the back of the closet until needed.

❧ 330 ❧

Babies and toddlers can easily wear clothes a little larger than their size. That way they will be able to wear them longer.

❧ 331 ❧

Empty baby wipe flip top containers make great sorters and storage bins for embroidery floss, zippers, buttons, thread, craft supplies, and more because they stack easily. Label the contents on the front of each container.

❧ 332 ❧

Nursing clothes are expensive to purchase. Next time you sew a jumper dress, put a six-inch zipper under the arms on both sides for a quick and discreet means of breast-feeding.

❧ 333 ❧

A regular nightgown can be easily transformed into a nursing gown. Cut two slits on either side of the breast. Finish the raw edges and sew snaps on to close the openings when not nursing the baby.

❧ 334 ❧

Teach your girls to sew. A simple-to-make and fun item for beginners is beanbags.

❧ 335 ❧

To taper the wrists of a blouse or dress, determine how much excess needs to be taken up to fit. Simply hand sew a snap on each sleeve, folding in the excess amount to make the sleeve fitted, if you are working on a garment without buttonholes. As the child grows, the snaps can be removed.

❧ 336 ❧

Wearing aprons or pinafores while working around the house protects your clothes from stains and excess wear. Denim makes a great outdoor play, gardening, and chores apron. Slip one on every time you go to the barn.

🦋 337 🦋

Here's a way to make new jumper dresses fit girls for two years instead of one. Make them one size larger. In the center back, close to the top, make a pleat (dart) by folding in a little fabric above the left shoulder blade toward the neck. Do the same thing to the right of the neck, folding in from the right shoulder and tack down. Follow this procedure again at the waistline seam. Tack into place and as your daughter grows, you can let out the pleats for expansion. And don't forget to provide a generous hem that will be let down the following year at the same time you let out the pleats.

🦋 338 🦋

The key to dressing for success in the country is to select clothes, fabrics, and patterns for practicality foremost. Function over frills.

🦋 *339* 🦋

Stay away from rayon and "dry clean only" items. Eliminate costly weekly drives to the cleaners.

🦋 *340* 🦋

Caught away from home without needle and thread? What do you do when the hem comes out of your dress or slacks? Tape it back into place until you have the time and supplies to hem.

🦋 *341* 🦋

Save empty cones of serger thread to wind lace, elastic, and binding around to keep the contents to your sewing basket from becoming an entangled mess.

🐜 *342* 🐜

The quickest way to change thread on your sewing machine or serger is to cut the thread already on your machine up close to the spool, allowing enough to tie on the next color to be used without unthreading the machine. Set the new spool on the machine and with a scrap piece of fabric under the needle, sew until the new color comes down and threads itself.

🐜 *343* 🐜

When working with basic thread colors, never thread just one bobbin. Thread at least three bobbins of the same thread color at a time. Colors to keep extra bobbins threaded are: black, white, beige, navy, and any others you use often.

🦜 *344* 🦜

Going on a trip? Keep luggage to a minimum. Pack your shoes in the same suitcase as your clothes. To keep the shoes from soiling the clothes, slide a large pair of old socks or a bread bag over the shoes.

🦜 *345* 🦜

Those flimsy nylon slip straps often get twisted and fall off the shoulder. Make your own comfortable slip out of batiste using a sleeveless dress pattern with a scoop neck. The ½" or ¾" straps are sewn as part of the bodice, thus staying in place. Add two darts to the bodice and you will have absolutely the most comfortable slip you've ever worn.

❧ 346 ❧

Simple reusable gift bags made of fabric instead of wrapping paper saves money. Using fabric scraps, take two like-size rectangles and sew up the two long sides and one short side. Hem the top. Sew eyelet, rickrack, or lace around the top or put a drawstring casing along the top. Slip the gift in and tie with ribbon, twine, or cord to complement your choice of fabric. A definite solution when wrapping odd-shaped items!

❧ 347 ❧

Altering Long Sleeves. A men's or boys' shirt can be shortened in the sleeves. Cut to desired length. Reattach the cuff. Take tucks in the sleeve as needed to fit the cuff.

❧ 348 ❧

Turn a dress shirt into a plain shirt and save the collar for an apron bow! Unbutton the dress shirt and turn the collar up. Cut the collar off close to the seam. With a seam ripper, open up the top seam at the neckline of the shirt. Usually, there's a small, stiff piece of fabric just inside. Remove and discard. Sew the neckline closed as it appeared previously. Now you have a banded collar shirt suitable for rural living. (Save the collars you cut off for the next project.)

❧ 349 ❧

A pointed collar makes a great, stiff bow that stays tied! (See photo on page 175.) Remember the jumper dress we turned into an apron? Here are ties for the sides you can make from collars. You'll need two identical pointed collars from two dress shirts. Fold each collar in half end to end and cut them in two. You now have two pieces for each side of the apron. Sew the straight

edge of a collar half to the front sides at the apron's waist and another half to both of the back sides until all four are attached. Stiff collars stay tied nicely in a bow. Great bow apron for an active girl.

🐦 350 🐦

A turtleneck dress makes a great cold weather blouse and slip! Wear a denim or corduroy jumper dress or skirt on top for added warmth. The top garment will need to be a little longer than the turtleneck dress underneath.

🦋 *351* 🦋

Need durable, quality blouses for outdoor work and play? Buy shirts for girls and ladies in the boys' and men's departments. There is a wider range of practical shirts built to last in denim, chambray, flannel, etc.

🦋 *352* 🦋

To estimate yardage of fabric or ribbon quickly, hold up to an exterior door opening. The standard exterior door is three feet wide, equivalent to one yard.

353

To sharpen a sewing machine needle, stitch through a piece of fine sandpaper.

354

Tired of tailor's chalk breaking? Here's something that works far better, and it's free, because you probably already have it in your home. It's soap. Once a bar of soap has been worn thin but not to the point of breaking, it is the ideal marking tool for sewing. Use it when cutting fabric, marking a hem, or altering.

355

Purchasing "cut-away" or "tear-away" stabilizers for use when embroidering can be expensive. Substitute a static cling dryer sheet instead.

❧ 356 ❧

This laundry product (cling-free dryer sheets) also comes in handy when sewing appliqués. Sew it to the front of the shape. Leave a slight opening and turn right side out.

❧ 357 ❧

To remove mistakes when machine embroidering, working from the back side, rub a disposable razor blade back and forth across the threads. Be careful not to cut down into the garment. After breaking the embroidery threads, carefully remove from the front with a seam ripper.

❧ *358* ❧

Tired of burning your finger when ironing narrow bias strips or other small items? An easy way to protect your index finger is to remove and wear the index finger from a knitted glove when ironing tiny items that you must hold in place.

Home Remedies and Good Health Practices

If you follow the latest reports and trends in healthy eating, you may find yourself off one food this year, then adding it to the recommended eating listing next year. I may be over simplifying it, but as I see it, if God gave it for us to eat and it is as near its natural state as possible to consume, it has to be the best of foods for us to eat! But, if we take the natural product and overprocess it, chemically alter it, and dye it, then it is no longer healthy eating! Fresh farm eggs, dairy goat milk and cheese, whole wheat bread baked fresh, garden produce, free range chickens, rabbit or beef, ripe berries, nuts and fruits and the physical work that goes into it all are what kept cancer at bay in our society long before highly processed fast food and frozen dinners from the grocer's freezer filled our shelves.

For several years now we've been learning about the usefulness of herbs medicinally and turn to herbs for remedy of mild maladies. Yet, when it came time to treat our tiny 5-pound baby boy, I did give it a second thought. A gentle woman encouraged me to pass the remedies on to our little preemie. And I remembered that home remedies are not a new fad. They have stood the test of time. Herbs were put on this earth for the service of man and so we shall continue in the use of the natural when we can. The very first herbal remedy I administered to our little son was red raspberry leaf tea for relief of diarrhea. It worked after the first or second dosage and continues to do so on occasion when it is needed for its gentle yet effective work.

359

The whey from fresh milk can be applied several times daily (for two to three days) to a minor wound to reduce infection.

360

A Nursing Herbal Tea Blend to stimulate breast milk production follows: Place 2 handfuls of blessed thistle dried leaves and 2 handfuls dried red raspberry leaves

along with 1 t. fennel seeds in a half-gallon jar and fill to the top with boiling water. Cap tightly and steep overnight or equivalent hours. Strain off the herbs and refrigerate tea. Drink a cup of tea during nursing times, up to 2 qt. per day. Heat each cup of tea close to boiling and let stand until cool enough to drink.

❧ *361* ❧

Researchers found that consuming as little as half a cup of caffeine coffee daily during the month before conceiving boosted miscarriage risk by 29%. Consuming the same amount during pregnancy boosted the risk by 15%. Each additional 100 milligrams of caffeine daily increased the risk by another 22%. That is the amount of caffeine in eight ounces of coffee, 16 ounces of tea or eight to 15 ounces of soft drinks that contain caffeine. (*Above Rubies* Nov. 1995, No. 44, AP wire service, December 11, 1993.)

❧ *362* ❧

Cayenne pepper stops bleeding. Apply directly to minor cuts.

❧ *363* ❧

Take garlic tablets 3 times daily to keep bugs from biting.

❧ *364* ❧

For insect stings and bites, crumble up the leaves of plantain and apply directly to the affected area.

❧ *365* ❧

Apple cider vinegar applied to a wasp sting helps stop the pain.

❧ *366* ❧

A paste of baking soda and water eases the pain of wasp stings.

❧ *367* ❧

Milkweed plant can be used to relieve itching of poison oak. Cut a piece of the stem and twist it back and forth until the juice oozes out. Apply directly to itching area.

☙ *368* ❧

Take vitamin A daily during spring and summer to repel chiggers (red bugs) from biting. This tip came from our land surveyor.

☙ *369* ❧

Drinking milk from free-range goats is said to build up an immunity to poison oak, etc., because goats consume poison oak in their diet.

☙ *370* ❧

Take 3 brewer's yeast tablets 3 times a day to increase breast milk production.

❧ *371* ❧

Brewer's yeast increases the energy level and is recommended for individuals undergoing cancer treatment. It's also great for moms with active babies and young children!

❧ *372* ❧

Tummy Ache Tea: Add 2 cups of water to a small pot and 1 bag apple herb tea. Place any combination of the following herbs and spices for the ailments present and simmer, never boil.

Whole cloves—a digestive aid, good for upset stomach and abdominal pain

Mint—fresh or dried, good for digestion

Fennel—good for stomachaches

Ginger—reduces fever and relieves vomiting

Marjoram—good for fever, flu, and vomiting

Nutmeg—Aids in relieving pain, indigestion, and diarrhea.

Savory—stomachaches

Strain the tea mixture after simmering, pour a cup, and sweeten to taste with honey!

❧ *373* ❧

Aloe is great for treating insect bites and minor burns. Keep a potted aloe plant close at hand. Break off a leaf, open to expose the gel, and rub directly on area needing relief.

❧ *374* ❧

Aloe is also a natural deodorant. Use it under the arms.

❧ *375* ❧

Witch hazel has natural deodorant qualities!

❧ *376* ❧

Sore Throat Gargle: Use lemon juice full strength for gargle or dilute lemon juice with equal amount of water and gargle frequently.

❧ *377* ❧

For relief of heartburn, add 1 t. lemon juice to half glass of water and drink.

❧ *378* ❧

Drink the juice of a lemon in a cup of water first thing in the morning before eating or drinking. Lemon juice is a good healer and blood purifier.

❧ *379* ☙

To treat acne, after washing and removing oils from the face, pat the face with lemon juice three times a day. Lemon juice aids in clearing the complexion!

❧ *380* ☙

Cough Suppressant: Mix apple cider vinegar and enough honey to taste in a small glass jar. Take a table-spoon as often as needed.

❧ *381* ☙

Lemon juice and honey relieves minor coughs, colds, and sore throats.

382

Garlic strengthens the body's immune system and is an infection fighter. Buy liquid garlic for young children.

383

Fenugreek and thyme both are used to lower cholesterol and to treat sinus congestion.

384

Echinacea is used to treat flu, colds, and infections. It has antibiotic and antiviral properties.

❧ 385 ❧

A frozen bag of peas makes a great ice pack! Ice packs are good for treating bumps, etc. to reduce swelling.

❧ 386 ❧

Suffering from food poisoning? Mix 2 T. activated charcoal powder with a glass of water or other beverage and drink.

❧ 387 ❧

Bee pollen has helped many arthritis sufferers.

☙ 388 ❧

Consuming large amounts of orange juice that was juiced while the oranges were still green may aggravate arthritis.

☙ 389 ❧

To encourage bowel movement, take cayenne pepper before bed. For more acute conditions, take cascara sagrada. For young children, include wheat bran in their daily diet.

☙ 390 ❧

Fevers in babies and young children are often associated with constipation. Keep the bowels moving nutritionally. Raw apple juice, prune juice, or elderberries often will stimulate the bowels to move sufficiently in children.

❧ *391* ❧

Activated charcoal (not the kind you use on the grill) can be applied to insect and spider bites and bee stings as a poultice to draw out the poisons. Moisten the charcoal with a little water and apply as a paste.

❧ *392* ❧

Tea tree oil (melaleuca) is a good topical treatment for minor abrasions and does not sting when applied to cuts, etc.

❧ 393 ❧

Red raspberry tea relieves diarrhea and is safe enough to give to babies.

❧ 394 ❧

Blackberry leaf tea is also a safe and effective remedy for diarrhea. Either can be combined with peppermint.

❧ 395 ❧

Red raspberry tea eases the discomfort of nausea from morning sickness.

❧ 396 ❧

To make herb tea: Heat one cup of water to boiling. Remove from heat and add 1 to 3 t. dried herbs (e.g., raspberry leaves). Use more if using fresh leaves. Allow to steep for several minutes. Sweeten with honey if desired.

❧ 397 ❧

Never give honey to a child under one year old!

❧ 398 ❧

Red raspberry tea is also good for strengthening the uterus for an upcoming delivery. Drinking too much early in pregnancy can cause spotting. Wait until your last trimester to drink it daily.

❧ 399 ☙

Chickweed is a natural source of vitamin C. It also reduces mucus in the lungs.

❧ 400 ☙

Don't neglect the significance of acquiring fresh air and sunshine in treatment of colds, etc. when weather permits.

❧ 401 ☙

Bite into a pepper that is too hot? Drink some cold milk for relief.

❧ *402* ❧

Blessed thistle increases the appetite.

❧ *403* ❧

Valerian is gentle, non-addictive, and relieves inner tension. Use to help relax the nerves and to relieve tension in the jaws after grinding or clenching your teeth during sleep.

❧ *404* ❧

Zinc lozenges usually contain zinc, vitamin C, and echinacea and are good for coughs and sore throats.

🐦 *405* 🐦

Beta carotene can be taken daily as a treatment for acne.

🐦 *406* 🐦

Make your own chapped lip balm. Melt 5 T. castor or quality vegetable oil, and 1 T. beeswax over low heat. Remove from heat and add 2 t. pure honey and blend well. When the balm is almost cooled, stir in 9 drops of tea tree (melaleuca) oil.

🐦 *407* 🐦

A comfrey sitz bath prompts healing of torn tissues after childbirth. Make a strong brew of comfrey tea and add it to 3" to 4" inches of very warm bath water.

❧ *408* ❧

Showers *only* for bathing for 2 to 3 weeks after birthing a baby. Do *not* bathe while sitting in the tub. Sitz baths are for soaking only.

❧ *409* ❧

The colostrum that a new mother's body produces before her milk comes in is rich in protein and other nutrients and contains antibodies that will protect her baby for up to six months! If you don't intend on breast-feeding, for your baby's sake do so the first week. The longer you nurse, the greater the benefit.

❦ *410* ❧

To reduce a fever blister, apply roll-on deodorant. The drying agents in deodorant dries up the fluid when applied several times daily for 1 to 2 days.

❦ *411* ❧

To relieve a sunburn, simmer several tea bags in a pot of water on the stove for ten minutes. Pour all into your bath water. Lie back and soak. The tannic acid in the tea soothes the burn.

❦ *412* ❧

Caught outdoors on a windy or sunny day? Here's relief for parched dry or chapped lips. Using your index finger, wipe the oils just behind the ears and rub on your lips for comfort.

❧ *413* ❧

Stir equal amounts of olive oil and vinegar together in a jar or bottle and apply when needed as a sunburn lotion.

❧ *414* ❧

For heat exhaustion, take sips of salt water (1 t. of salt per glass).

❧ *415* ❧

Breathing in salt air is recommended for those suffering sinus problems. Take a walk on the beach.

❧ 416 ❧

Eating yogurt with live active cultures, acidophilus, adds friendly bacteria needed to those suffering from yeast infections.

❧ 417 ❧

Make your own saline nasal spray. Dissolve ¼ t. of salt in an 8-oz. glass of warm water. Use a clean medicine dropper to put a few drops of the solution inside the nostrils. Follow with the use of a suction bulb when administering to babies for a stuffy nose. Saline solution helps sinus infection.

❧ 418 ❧

Reduce puffy, swollen eyes with a damp tea bag held against the eye area.

🦋 *419* 🦋

Apply egg whites to a minor burn for quick relief.

🦋 *420* 🦋

Cornstarch can be easily applied to creases and folds in the baby's skin with a powder puff during diaper changes to prevent diaper rash, especially during the hot season.

🦋 *421* 🦋

Cornstarch gives cool, dry comfort to the body, preventing heat rash.

☙ 422 ❧

Basic Herbal Tincture
1 bottle Everclear Alcohol
1 bottle distilled or spring water (same quantity as alcohol)
6 oz. dried herbs, cut and sifted. (If working with fresh, double the amount.) Cut and bruise well. Put herb, alcohol, and water in a jar with a tight lid. Shake daily for 12 days. Let rest for 2 days or longer. Strain and put into a dark bottle. Generally, 1 tsp. tincture = 3 capsules of herbs.

☙ 423 ❧

Suffering from a cold? Nasal congestion? Stay off dairy products until well. Both dairy foods and orange juice increase mucus in the body. Choose goat's milk over cow's milk and grapefruit juice over orange juice.

❧ *424* ❧

White rice and white flours create excess mucus in the body. Instead, cook with brown rice and freshly ground whole wheat flour.

❧ *425* ❧

Healing Herbal Salve Recipe:

1½ c. olive oil or enough to cover the herbs (may use lard, canola, or peanut oil)

1 T. glycerin

1½ t. tincture of benzoin (from a pharmacy)

½ c. herbs (combination of comfrey, plantain, and sage)

1½ t. dried powdered goldenseal root mixed to a paste with 3 T. oil

1 to 2 oz. pure beeswax

1 t. vitamin E or A (oil or capsule)

Directions:
Cook herbs in the oil over low heat, in a crock-pot on low or oven at 250° F. for 5 to 6 hours. Strain and return to pot, adding the glycerin and tincture of benzoin. Melt in the beeswax and vitamin E or A. Pour in jars and label.

🦋 *426* 🦋

Lip Balm Recipe:
½ c. almond oil
¼ c. cocoa butter
¼ c. coconut oil
1 T. pure honey
2 oz. pure beeswax
1½ T. natural flavoring (vanilla, almond oil, etc.)

Directions:
Heat oil and stir in cocoa butter and coconut oil. Stir in the honey and wax and test for firmness. Add a little more wax if needed. Then, stir in the flavoring. Pour

into little round containers. Allow to cool and harden before using.

427

To preserve large stocks of herbal salves or lip balms containing oils and fats, store in jars in a root cellar, the refrigerator, or freezer until needed.

428

Plantain (*Plantago* genus) is great for treating insect bites, bee stings, and poison ivy. If you are outside when someone is stung, pick a few leaves from the plant and bruise. (Twist in your hands or chew in your mouth.) Then apply to the sting.

The astringent action in the plantain quickly draws out the poison as it pulls the tissue together, thus reducing the pain within seconds. If you apply plantain soon enough, you may avoid any swelling as well. Swelling is the result of the body's defense system reacting to the poisonous sting. Thus, it is also a good anti-inflammatory.

❦ *429* ❦

Plantain Tincture

Fill a glass jar with ⅓ plantain and ⅔ apple cider vinegar. Keep in a dark, cool place for 3 weeks, shaking it every day or so. After 3 weeks, strain the vinegar tincture and store in a jar with a dropper or a squeeze top container for easy use. This tincture is especially useful in treating blemishes on the face. Plantain pulls out the poison of the blemish and will often lift the discoloration around the blemishes as well.

❧ *430* ❧

For good oral hygiene, replace your toothbrush every three months, and *every* month during the winter flu and cold season. Bacteria on toothbrushes can cause sore throat pain!

❧ *431* ❧

Athlete's foot powder can be made at home by combining 1 cup boric acid powder, 0.67 cups talc, and 0.33 cups sodium thiosulfate (photography supply). Sprinkle on feet, work between the toes.

❧ *432* ❧

Herbal Cough Syrup
Ingredients needed: 2 oz. powdered or cut herbs,

1 quart pure water boiled down to 1 pt., 2 oz. honey, and or glycerin and cheesecloth.

Directions:

Boil 1 quart water and herbs for comfort and flavor in your desired combinations (comfrey, anise seeds, fennel seed, Irish moss, wild cherry bark, licorice). Boil until mixture measures one pint. Strain through cheesecloth.

While still warm, add 2 oz. glycerin and/or honey to liquid. Mix thoroughly. Store in bottles and label.

🦋 433 🦋

Dry Glycerin Rose Gel

Mix 5 t. gelatin with 2¼ c. hot water. Cool to lukewarm. Then add 3 T. glycerin and a few drops of oil-based scent (rose, lavender, etc.). Store in a glass jar. Apply to dry skin: elbows, heels, etc. as needed.

❧ 434 ❧

Have a headache? Reach for a glass of water first instead of aspirin. Headaches are often a sign of a need for water.

❧ 435 ❧

Earaches are a common childhood ailment. A safe earache remedy is to put a few drops of warm (never hot) garlic oil directly into the ear. Also, massage some of the garlic oil around the ear. If you don't keep garlic oil on hand, warm olive oil with minced garlic and strain. Repeat as needed.

❧ 436 ❧

Make Garlic Oil. It's easy. Simply peel cloves of fresh garlic and place in a glass jar. Pour in enough olive oil to cover. Store in the refrigerator. Remove as needed.

❧ 437 ❧

Most everyone has heard that cranberry juice is a remedy for urinary tract infections. When cranberries are in season, buy several bags and juice. Keep some stored in the freezer to relieve the burning sensation when fresh cranberries aren't available. And drink plenty of fluid to flush the kidneys.

❧ 438 ❧

When we become ill, vitamin C is one of the first vitamins our body is depleted of. A friend eliminated all the symptoms of mononucleosis in her daughter in just two days with megadoses of vitamin C. How do you know when your body has had too much vitamin C? Your body will tell you. Diarrhea will occur. During any illness that lasts more than a few days such as pneumonia, strep throat, or mono and especially when antibiotics are taken, it is important to rebuild your immune system.

⚜ *439* ⚜

Are you among those females that crave chocolate just prior to your monthly menses? Combat this craving by eating dark green leafy vegetables. Your body is signaling a vitamin deficiency.

⚜ *440* ⚜

Severe cramps during menstruation are often a sign of poor eating habits and stress. If you suffer from severe cramps, try staying off processed foods and chocolate. Instead, eat plenty of dark green vegetables. Then welcome the improvement. It's a small sacrifice to pay to relieve yourself of monthly discomfort.

✸ *441* ✸

Suffering from clogged sinuses? Eat spicy foods! Often a spicy Mexican or Indian dish is all it will take to clear clogged sinus passages.

✸ *442* ✸

Do you frequently suffer from heartburn? Relief is at hand! Add a tablespoon of raw apple cider vinegar to a glass of water and sip it while eating.

✸ *443* ✸

Bedwetting problems in the house? Cornsilk is a natural remedy. Dry your own from harvested corn. Store and use to make an herbal tea when needed.

❧ 444 ❧

To make an infusion, pour a cup of boiling water over one or two teaspoons of herbs. Allow the herbs to steep in the hot water for several minutes. Then strain.

For a stronger brew, simmer 2 t. herbs in a cup of water for 30 minutes.

❧ 445 ❧

Childhood and nosebleeds often go hand-in-hand. When a sudden nosebleed occurs sit quietly with the head tilted back. Press the nose firmly at the nostrils with a damp cloth.

❧ 446 ❧

Feel faint? Sit with your head between your knees and breathe deeply. Apply cold compress to the face, and neck. If this doesn't help, fill a bath tub 1" deep with cold water, disrobe, and lie back.

🦋 447 🦋

To remove a splinter, wash the area or blot with an alcohol swab. Sterilize the tweezers by running back and forth across a flame. If deeply embedded, sterilize a straight pin and poke through the skin at the center of the splinter. Grasp and pull out with tweezers when splinter is close to or just above the skin.

🦋 448 🦋

Dehydration is a dying person's friend. Forcing a person approaching death to drink fluids or take an IV only prolongs his agony and postpones the inevitable.

✌ 449 ✌

Hold a mirror close to the mouth when you need to confirm death. The smallest trace of breath will fog up the mirror.

✌ 450 ✌

Stomach cramps more than you can bear? Take deep breaths and try to relax. With face down, on the bed, draw your knees up to your chest in the fetal position. If this doesn't help, apply an ice pack to the lower abdomenal area to help numb the pain.

✌ 451 ✌

Studies show that diets high in squash consumption can lower the risk of cancer. See cooking section for directions on cooking pumpkin.

❧ 452 ❧

Hanging sheets and towels, cloth diapers and clothes on an outdoor clothesline is beneficial to your health. Sunshine disinfects germs.

❧ 453 ❧

Consuming artificial sweeteners cause the body to crave sugar.

Refer to the Barnyard, Animal section for specific remedies for livestock and pets.

Home Furnishings

Our home is our place of refuge, a place where one can relax, find comfort, cheer, and warmth. How we care for the home and furnish it helps set the mood, the pace, and the rules therein. If we furnish our home with porcelain, china, and crystal accessories on table, counter, and shelf tops, then we are establishing a showplace. An untouchable, hands-off room makes the things in the room more important than the people that the room should serve!

When people come to our home, we hope it will feel like going to Grandma's. Grandma's, or Grannie as we called ours down south was always high on the top ten list of favorite people and places to visit. A place where you can truly relax in a comfortable chair with a glass of iced tea, and plenty of enjoyable conversation. A visitor to Grannie's was instantly welcomed by the warmth and glow from the fireplace and Grannie's wonderful hospitality. Equally as charming were homemade rag rugs positioned underfoot on the heartwood pine floors that glowed after a buff and polish with paste wax. And if you were fortunate enough to be an overnight guest, nothing felt more comfortable than to slide beneath a pile of handmade quilts made from the scraps of Grannie's dresses. Further sinking cozily into the soft feather mattress, oh, how hard it was in the morning to crawl out of a perfectly cozy bed. Through the night, the bedrooms were kept a little cool on purpose so you'd sleep better, she'd say. I think it was because Grannie wanted to make sure that her quilts didn't get kicked off onto the floor and certainly because she'd seen hard times and hadn't forgotten them. In hard times or when life's a breeze, home is the best place to be!

❧ 454 ❧

Eliminate replacing box springs. Build a plywood box frame with a top and sides to fit directly on the top of the bed frame in place of box springs. It shouldn't need replacing. The mattress will rest right on top of the constructed box frame.

❧ 455 ❧

Don't throw wallpaper scraps away. Using leftover remnants or a single roll of wallpaper cut stenciled shapes to create a wall border. Animal shapes make a nice wall border addition to a child's room.

❧ 456 ❧

Save money when decorating. Instead of purchasing stencils, use cookie cutters you already have on hand.

Trace around the outer edge and fill in with paint as desired when making borders or adorning furniture, etc.

🦋 457 🦋

Cut out specific images imprinted on wallpaper, such as farm animals, flowers or vegetables, etc. to decorate picture frames, hat boxes or even the backs of wooden or wicker benches and other desired pieces of furniture. When using on furniture, spray a craft sealer on the design to keep it looking fresh.

🦋 458 🦋

Use feather mattresses on top of a regular mattress for added coziness and warmth. They are especially comfortable when sick and temporarily bedridden.

❧ *459* ❧

Make window valances or throw pillows out of large dinner napkins, or even bandanas. Make curtains from kitchen towels.

❧ *460* ❧

A quilted bedspread can be used to make a tailored bed skirt. Coordinate with existing bed coverings. Cut to size and make throw pillows from the excess fabric for the finishing touch.

❧ *461* ❧

If the top of a small wooden table or tray is excessively worn, try covering with broken pieces of old china, ceramic dishes, or ceramic tile. Grout in between pieces. A fresh new face, perfect for use on the porch.

❧ 462 ❧

To make a bedspread and pillow sham ensemble for a daybed, use one queen-size bedspread. Cut to size and use the excess to make two large pillow shams to go across the back.

❧ 463 ❧

An old-fashioned wash basin makes a good fruit bowl display. If you have a stand and pitcher to go along, load it all up with fresh fruit and nuts and nut crackers. It creates a visual welcome when receiving guests.

❧ 464 ❧

Desire a kitchen or dining room decoration? Display your plates. Purchase plate hangers and hang one or an arrangement of your favorite keepsake plates on the wall. These are less expensive than paintings and are functional. Or, hang a wooden plate rack or shelf to attractively display the cups and plates that you use daily.

Old jeans make great pillow fabric for porch furniture. Cut off each leg. Turn each tube inside out. Stitch the top part closed. Fill with old rags, pantyhose, or fiberfill, leaving 3" inches free. Gather in your hand 3" up from the opening. Secure with a tight rubber band. Cover rubber band with a bow of twine or braided cording. This will create a fan effect on one edge. The denim pockets can be sewn on throw pillows. Stuff pocket with a bandana.

❧ 466 ❧

For efficient living, eliminate figurines from your decorating. Replace with usable items such as an antique serving tray, cookie jars, canisters. For less clutter and time spent in cleaning, the items in your home should be as functional and practical as they are attractive.

❧ 467 ❧

Adopt this philosophy: "The house and its furnishings should serve you instead of you serving the house."

❧ 468 ❧

A rustic toilet paper holder can be made from a thin but sturdy twig. Cut 6 inches wider than a roll of toilet pa-

per. Tie a piece of thin rope or durable twine onto each end and hang from the center of the twine with a cup hook.

⚘ 469 ⚘

Old weathered barn wood makes handsome rustic picture frames.

❧ *470* ❧

If you live in the warmer regions of America, you can gather your own natural stuffing for upholstery and pillows. Spanish moss, nicknamed vegetable horsehair, is often found hanging in oak trees or on the ground beneath. It is used commercially for this purpose. Chiggers live in Spanish moss, so beware.

❧ *471* ❧

Give standard picture frame matting that rustic flair. Cut burlap slightly larger than the outer perimeter of the matting. Apply glue to the matting and lay the burlap in place to cover. Score an X across the center of the burlap (in the center opening of the mat) with a sharp craft knife. This will leave 4 V flaps to fold to the back of the matting and glue down. Trim the excess burlap from the outer perimeter and your mat is ready for the barn wood frame. (Bandanas and calico can also be glued to standard matting for a country touch.)

❧ 472 ❧

Burlap can be glued to trays and flower pots and make quaint cottage curtains when tied back with twine or raffia bows.

❧ 473 ❧

Dual functioning furniture is a smart way to go to make every foot count in the home. Select plans for or purchase furniture that can serve two useful purposes or is transitional, thus reducing space consumed and quantity of furniture required.

❧ 474 ❧

An upright trunk makes a great bedside table and provides an inside storage space 3-feet deep.

❧ *475* ❧

A coffee table occupies a substantial amount of space in the living area of a home. Consider making your next coffee table a cedar chest. Use a sheet of acrylic on top to protect the surface.

❧ *476* ❧

Benches, whether used at the breakfast table, in a great room, or on the front porch could very well be housing goods too. Incorporate benches with storage boxes below.

❧ *477* ❧

Next time you purchase or build an island in the kitchen, consider one with two hinged drop leaf pieces on two sides. Great place to serve dinner for two. Pull up two stools and there's always room for more. Also perfect to have on hand to accommodate an overflow from your dining table. Roll the island into the dining room.

❧ 478 ❧

When the baby bed is no longer needed, remove the rollers and the sliding side rail. Fill with bolster pillows and you'll have a cozy mini daybed for young children to curl up with their favorite story book!

❧ 479 ❧

Since baby beds are up off the floor, make good use of the space below. Place a long drawer from a discarded dresser underneath the baby bed and fill it up with clothes, sheets, blankets, etc. A bed skirt keeps the drawer and clothes out of view.

🦋 *480* 🦋

A flat dressing table with a hinged lid can be used from birth to adulthood. Place a terry changing pad on top of the table for a diaper changing station. When diapers are no more, remove the pad and store brushes, combs, and stationery, and other writing supplies for a desk and dressing table combination.

🦋 *481* 🦋

With a laminated counter top and 2 oak 2-drawer file cabinets on either side, serving as the base, you'll have an attractive sewing/craft center or an office desk and files.

❧ 482 ❧

Allow a quiet space in the home for a library. Book shelves, desk, and a beanbag chair for little ones are all that's needed to start one and a few books or tapes as well!

❧ 483 ❧

When family members come in from chores and working outside, it's essential to have a mud room area with sink, a bench for taking off and storing boots beneath, and a rack for hanging hats and jackets. This helps the rest of the house stay clean longer.

❧ 484 ❧

Furniture and household accessories with all the charm of a country homestead can be constructed from washboards. They can be painted for a more subtle appearance.

❧ 485 ❧

Consider using a washboard for a door to your medicine cabinet.

❧ 486 ❧

Hang a washboard on the wall with a dowel rod inserted horizontally at the base of the legs and you've got a charming towel rack for the laundry room.

❧ 487 ❧

Use two washboards as legs when making a small bench, table, or mini bookcase combined with lumber.

488

Space under basement stairs is often wasted. Frame in the space. Put up some plywood for an extra storage closet.

489

Need a secret storage compartment in the house? Who'd check under the bottom step on a staircase?

490

Need more shelf space? Put shelves over windows, doorways, and around the upper portion of walls.

491

Piano keys should be exposed to light during the day, but not to direct sunlight. Darkness hastens the natural yellowing of real ivory. Pianos should be tuned three times a year.

492

Cute country curtain tiebacks can be easily assembled by stringing old wooden thread spools onto twine.

493

Reverse the position of floor rugs every month to distribute the wear evenly.

❦ *494* ❦

Flip your mattresses and turn them around every couple of months to avoid sags.

❦ *495* ❦

No need to buy curtain rods again when you go rustic. If you have saplings at hand, you've got a potential rustic curtain rod. Choose a branch or sapling that has a fork in it. You'll need two of these to support the rod. Cut each branch about 3" beneath the fork. With a drill, screw both rod supports to the wall in two places about an inch apart. Select a complimentary "rod" from the same tree species. Saw to length needed. Curtains with tab tops lend well to this type window rod treatment.

❧ *496* ☙

Here's a conversation piece for displaying your pots, pans, and cooking utensils. Acquire an old wagon wheel and suspend it from the ceiling over your cook-stove by 4 chains. Put several S hooks on the spokes to hang your cooking ware.

❧ *497* ☙

Cups taking up too much room in the cupboard? Place cup hooks underneath a cabinet or on a thin strip of wood mounted to the wall horizontally.

❧ *498* ☙

Display heirloom quilts with a rustic flair. Acquire an old wooden ladder and hang on the wall. Perfect backdrop. Use a smaller wooden ladder for hanging towels in the bathroom.

🎋 *499* 🎋

Old quilts make lovely table coverings. Find an old quilt, but most of it is too worn to use? Cut out the squares that are in good condition and make into throw pillows or place mats.

🎋 *500* 🎋

Have an old sewing machine cabinet (or writing desk) not in use? It's perfect for transforming into a server for your dining room or a dressing table for the bedroom. Cover the top with a thin sheet of plywood and the fabric of your choice. Make a fabric skirt for the base, gathering the fabric for fullness. Tack the skirt to the plywood or use double stick tape. To add the finishing touches, wrap braided cording around the skirt top to conceal the tacks and have a sheet of glass or acrylic cut to fit the top.

❦ *501* ❦

Worn boots make great bird feeders. Fill with a bouquet of dried flowers and seed pods and hang by the shoe strings on a sturdy tree close to the house.

❦ *502* ❦

If you can find an old double-deck, metal chicken laying unit that has multiple round openings, it makes an adorable storage system for most any room in the house with available wall space. The wooden strip along the bottom can hold S hooks or cup hooks to hang cups or equipment from. The bins could display your plates or canning goods antique country style!

❧ *503* ❧

Do you have a straight-back chair that needs a new seat bottom? Try tightly interweaving men's neckties. Use a staple gun to affix the basket weave ties to the underside of the chair bottom.

❧ *504* ❧

Here's the perfect candle holders for your log home. I call them log lights. Cut from a branch 3 pieces in grad-

uated heights: 8", 6", and 4". Measure the base of long tapered candles. Using the correct drill bit, drill a well in the center of each branch to hold the 3 candles in place. Nestle a grouping of three log lights on either side of a fireplace mantel for rustic romance.

🦎 505 🦎

To make your own Yule log light, saw a branch about 9" long. Cut a piece off one side to serve as the flat bottom. Drill three holes into the top (bark side) of the branch to fit tapered candles. For further decoration, use a glue gun to affix tiny pinecones, cinnamon sticks tied with raffia and the balls from a sweetgum tree around the candles.

❧ 506 ❧

Are the louvers in the window shutters broken? Remove the center louver portion and replace with enough horizontal pieces of twigs cut to size and nailed to the back of the shutter to fill in the opening. Paint or stain the shutter to complement the color of the twig pieces.

❧ 507 ❧

Wire lampshade frames can be transformed into original baskets for housing a potted plant when turned upside down and woven with grapevines. And of course, you can always use the lampshade frame interwoven with grapevines as a rustic lampshade.

❧ *508* ❧

Ready to change oil paintings or prints? You just can't sell a painting through the newspaper unless it is by a known artist. It's too hard to describe. And if you try to sell it in a yard sale, you won't get anything for it. So, here's a creative solution that worked for a couple we know. Approach a local restaurant or even a small hospital or medical office that your paintings would compliment. Ask it they would hang the artwork in a public room for viewing with the price affixed. For doing so, they get a free decoration and you can work out a percentage to compensate them for showing and selling the painting.

❧ *509* ❧

Has the life gone out of your mattress? No money for a new one? Extend the life of your mattress by purchasing an egg crate foam mattress covering. It's much cheaper than buying a new mattress, usually around $12.00, yet adds plush comfort to your bedding for at least another year.

Barnyard, Animals, and By-Products

It's not a farm without animals! And when you have animals, you have no need for television or commercial entertainment. Have you ever watched chickens chase flying insects around the yard? What a sight! It's better than any cartoon! Goats, chickens, mules, and the like are sure to keep you busy, amused, permanently enrolled in the classroom of continuing education, happy, sad, but most often glad. As another spring comes and the little ones are born, it makes all the work seem worthwhile. Nothing is sweeter or prettier than a young kid. Goats are pretty when they are just an hour old and all cleaned up. She'll cuddle up to you, even lay her head on your shoulder, stretching her slender neck for you to rub as she coos like a precious baby.

When they get a little bigger they can jump sideways and twist in the air, especially when there are two at play. Once when my folks were visiting, they were sleeping in our popup camper in the yard. In the early morning hours, Mother awoke to a loud clanging sound. She was startled by this of-

fensive noise and being a city gal, feared that thieves were making off with Lowell's tool box. She cautiously opened the camper door to inspect the situation, only to find that a few of the young goats decided it was time to play. They were running up and down the metal grain elevator outside the old barn. Taking turns jumping off, then playing king of the mountain, butting the other kids off was their early morning recreation. She was delighted by their play and crawled back into bed, leaving the camper door ajar so she could watch the frolic. All fears faded in the merriment. Here in the country, being awakened at night, at times, by some nocturnal animal, it is relieving to remember that opossums don't steal cars and coyotes don't break down barn doors!

❧ *510* ❧

Your old wooden ladder could also serve as a chicken roost. But if your chickens are like ours, they'll all want the top rung. Mount the ladder horizontally on the wall at an angle.

❧ *511* ❧

Use an empty soda bottle for feeding kids or lambs. After cleaning the bottle, add milk or replacer and put a lamb-size rubber nipple on top. Works great.

❧ 512 ❧

Cut a car tire in half. Use each half as a feeder or watering tray.

❧ 513 ❧

Free Dog Food. When butchering (deer, goat, beef, or pork) time rolls around, don't forget to save the scraps that won't be used for human consumption for dog food. Place the scraps in pint-size canning jars, add water, and can at 10 lbs. pressure for 90 minutes.

❧ 514 ❧

More Free Dog Food. When acquiring tallow from the grocery store or butcher, you may find plenty of meat left with the fat. Separate the meat from the fat. Place meat in canning jars and can as previously noted for dog food. (Most likely it has been left at room temperature too long for human consumption.)

🦜 515 🦜

A high protein treat for your dog that is free and usually thrown away is hoofs! When it's time to trim the horse or mule hoofs, save them for the dog.

🦜 516 🦜

Peppermint oil is a deterrent for mites in beehives.

🦜 517 🦜

If you find a dead animal such as a fox, etc. on the side of the road in the summertime and are tempted to pick it up for its fur hide, don't! The bacteria that multiplies so rapidly in any dead carcass in hot, humid conditions could kill you if it penetrates a cut on your skin!

❧ *518* ❧

Summer is not a good time to tan hides. Flies will lay eggs on hides left outside for any period of time and maggots will soon ruin the animal skin.

❧ *519* ❧

The best time to tan an animal hide is right away.

❦ 520 ❦

If you want to wait and tan a hide later, it's easy to do with a freezer and salt. Cover the flesh side of the pelt with plenty of coarse salt. Fold the hide over in half, flesh-to-flesh. Never let the hair touch the flesh as it will cause the hair to fall out. Then, roll it up, place in a plastic garbage bag, tie shut, and store in the freezer until ready to start the tanning process. A salted hide will not freeze hard even in a chest freezer.

❦ 521 ❦

Never store a tanned fur (rug, coat, etc.) in plastic!

❦ 522 ❦

Every animal has enough brains to tan itself.

❧ 523 ❧

You can purchase pig brains from the grocery store or butcher and use for brain tanning various animal hides.

❧ 524 ❧

Salt is used in the process of tanning hides. An economical salt for tanning is water softening salt pellets. A 50-lb. bag costs just a few dollars!

❧ 525 ❧

Every farmstead needs guineas to help decrease the tick and bug population.

❧ 526 ❧

Chickens do their share of bug eating when left to free range.

❧ 527 ❧

Goat Breeding Tip. One cup of apple cider vinegar to 3 gallons of warm water beginning 6 weeks before breeding will help generate more doe eggs, getting up to 75% doe kids.

❧ 528 ❧

Planning on using a buck goat for meat? Neuter by banding or other castration in the first month. The meat will be fine for eating after sufficient weight gain.

❧ 529 ❧

De-horn goats for their safety and yours. De-horning is best done during the 3rd through 5th days, when the buds first appear on the top of the head.

❧ 530 ❧

A coffee filter makes a great milk strainer. No need to purchase special or expensive equipment.

❧ 531 ❧

When feeding goat milk to human babies, supplement with folic acid to compensate for the milk's deficiency.

532

Don't let children, or anything else for that matter, chase your chickens or they won't lay eggs.

533

Try raising rabbits. Rabbit meat can be substituted in almost any chicken recipe. Rabbits are by far faster to butcher than chickens. Rabbits don't require as much space to raise as chickens. They multiply faster and their meat is even lower in fat content!

534

Beeswax is used to make many things, from lip salves to candles. When removing it from the beehive, an easy and natural method for cleaning a large bulk of wax is to let your bees do the work. Set the wax on a large tray next to your bees. Within 24 to 36 hours, the wax should be clean. The bees will remove any remaining particles of honey, etc.

❧ 535 ❧

Wood ashes or tobacco have been used to worm horses.

❧ 536 ❧

Make a pet pillow for your dog or cat and fill with cedar shavings. Don't forget to use a zipper in the construction so you can wash the fabric and change the shavings from time to time.

❧ 537 ❧

Line the floor of the dog house with cedar shavings or chips to deter fleas and other insects. Shovel cedar shavings into the horse stalls for fly control. To acquire large amounts of cedar shavings, contact a local sawmill.

❧ 538 ❧

Here's how the old-timers removed skunk odor from the farm dog. Give the dog a bath in tomato sauce. Then conclude with a bath of shampoo and a sprinkle of baking soda. Scrub well and rinse.

❧ *539* ❧

Man's best friend could be your neighbors' worst enemy. Keep your dog on your property unless accompanied by you. When harmless dogs get together with other dogs they have been known to attack and viciously kill livestock.

❧ *540* ❧

To catch a chicken, wait until dusk or dark when they are less likely to run away. Hold up a broom stick or branch (thick enough for the chicken to get a good grip) close to the place the chicken is perched. The chicken will step right off its perch and onto the stick you are holding. Then carry the chicken on the stick wherever you want.

541

Break a chicken from eating her eggs. Take a cracked egg or slightly crack one yourself. Remove some of the yolk with a syringe. Replace it with hot pepper sauce. Reseal the crack with mayonnaise. Set out in a conspicuous spot and it'll be hot tamales for the guilty hen!

542

To relieve a goat from overeating, pour a cup of vegetable oil into its mouth. Bloat can kill a goat. (This method relieved a greedy dairy goat who'd helped herself to a bag of green apples.)

543

To encourage young hens to lay, place an egg or an egg gourd in the laying box.

❧ 544 ❧

Only want to milk once a day? It's simple. Lock the dairy goat or cow up alone at night. Milk in the morning and turn the doe loose with kids for the rest of the day.

❧ 545 ❧

Turkeys can be hard to raise. Put a young turkey with a good mothering chicken. She'll take care of the rest, literally taking it under wing at night, up to the point that the turkey has grown to equal her size!

❧ 546 ❧

A cat or two is vital on the farm in keeping the rodent population away from the animal feed.

❦ 547 ❦

Wanting to start small with livestock? When purchasing social animals with a built-in flocking nature, it's best to purchase more than one. Examples are goats and sheep. They hate to be alone. It is cute to have a little kid follow you around when it's little, but it can be a serious nuisance when big! Your guests may not appreciate a 6-month-old goat jumping in their lap on the porch!

❦ 548 ❦

When buying an animal from another farm it is good to ask what type of feed they have been giving the animal and continue with it. Any changes in feed should be done gradually, especially in rabbits, sheep, goats, cattle, deer, and buffalo and other ruminating animals.

☙ *549* ☙

Goats like their water clean. If fresh running water isn't available via a spring, make sure the goat's water bucket gets changed upon first sight of debris.

☙ *550* ☙

Shortly after a kid or lamb is born, place rubbing alcohol or 7% iodine into a small medicine cup. Dip the newborn kid or lamb's umbilical cord in the alcohol cup. The umbilical cord will act like a wick and draw up the liquid, keeping down infection.

☙ *551* ☙

Goat milk is delicious and the preferred milk in most countries. It should never taste goaty unless you keep the buck in the herd with the does. P.S. Bucks don't smell bad all the time, just during breeding season.

❧ 552 ❧

Want to dehorn an adult goat? You can saw off an inch a month.

❧ 553 ❧

Need to stop bleeding during dehorning cattle or goats? Try cobwebs, farmers have been using them for years! Cobwebs can usually be found in the henhouse or barn.

❧ 554 ❧

Donkeys are often put in the field to protect goats from coyote attacks.

❧ 555 ❧

If your dairy animal starts producing off-taste milk, check the pasture for wild onions and garlic. Are you using anything other than a stainless steel bucket to

collect the milk? Are you washing the udder and teats with soap and water and drying them before starting to milk? Are you keeping the stalls and milking Stanchion free of manure? Are you cooling the milk as soon as it has been strained? And lastly, never mix warm milk with chilled milk.

🐦 556 🐦

Just moved and haven't had a chance to build the dog house yet? To provide a quick, temporary dog house, tack a tarp over a sawhorse, leaving an opening in the front. For larger dogs, set the sawhorse up on cement blocks or pallets.

🐦 557 🐦

Another quick, temporary animal shelter can be made by stringing up a clothesline 4' or 5' feet off the ground. Drape a tarp over the clothesline and anchor it to the ground with rocks, blocks, or tent stakes. Place a wood pallet inside to provide protection from a wet ground.

❧ 558 ☙

Raising rabbits? Then, you should be raising fishing worms as well. Place boxes beneath the rabbit cages with earthworms and they'll go to work converting the droppings into casts that can be used like potting soil fertilizer for plants and garden. Besides this benefit, the rabbitry should have less odor, less clean-up involved. The worms do the work and you'll have fishing worms to sell too!

❧ 559 ☙

What do you do in winter when the watering system to your caged rabbits freezes up? Fill Dixie cups with water and set out to freeze. Pop the frozen ice out and put one in the cage for each rabbit. While you're waiting for the Dixie cups to freeze, check outside for icicles (especially if you have a cave entrance). Icicles are similar in shape to a carrot. Rabbits love them, can hold them quite well, and enjoy chomping the wet treat!

560

Clip your goat's long beard in winter to avoid its getting wet and freezing.

561

On exceptionally cold mornings, provide warm water for the animals to drink.

562

Renewing Feather Pillows. To renew musty-smelling feathers, place in a pillowcase tied at the top and submerge in a borax and boiling water bath. Dunk the pillowcase in the borax water for several minutes to ensure complete saturation of the feathers. Drip dry on outdoor clothesline. Fluff when dry and transfer the dry feathers to new pillows or clean ticking.

563

Do your chickens quit laying eggs in winter? Get them laying again with Grandmother's old secret. Feed your hens dried red hot peppers. Do so for about 3 days in a row and they should start laying again.

❦ 564 ❦

More than one person should be aware of the feeding, milking routines on the farm. It's a good idea to keep written records posted in the barn of what and how often you feed each animal as well as any other special instructions. It will help the farm continue to run smoothly, and the animals to stay in good condition, in your absence.

❦ 565 ❦

Need to catch an ornery pig? Put a bucket over his head and lead him backwards.

❦ 566 ❦

During the processing of meat chickens, keep the birds in cool water after scalding. Add cider vinegar to the water in the holding tank (ice chest, etc.) to keep down bacteria formation during processing.

567

If you think that deer meat is tough and chewy, try canning your next deer. Canning tenderizes the meat tremendously. Pressure can ground meat or chunks in canning jars with water and salt for 90 minutes at 10 lbs. pressure.

568

For those tough old birds or rabbits, grind the meat, then pressure can. Use meat in casseroles, barbecue, or salads.

🦚 569 🦚

Spread the manure from the barn stalls (rabbits, cows, goats, horses, mules) on next spring's planting site and plow it under or add it to an existing compost heap.

🦚 570 🦚

The most durable leather to use for moccasins is buffalo or elk. Deerskin is suited for moccasin-type bedroom slippers only.

🦚 571 🦚

Free range chickens laying their eggs everywhere but in their nests? Lock the hens up in their house for several days with ample food and water. Fill each nest with hay or straw. Provide a wire pen from the door outside, so they can obtain fresh air, sunshine, insects, etc. daily during their training session. Keep penned until they start laying eggs. When allowed to resume free ranging, they should come back to the nest to lay.

572

Rid your sheds and barns of mice without poisons. Put 2" or 3" of water in a bucket and set beside a counter. Drop a scant amount of corn in too, if you like. Mice will fall into the bucket and drown.

573

Looking to buy a lamb or young sheep? Examine the teeth. If it has a full mouth of teeth, it's at least four years old. The two center milk teeth are replaced by permanent teeth at 12 to 14 months. Another pair of teeth appear each year until four years of age, when the sheep finally has a full set.

❧ *574* ❧

Sheep meat flavors vary with the breed of sheep and its age. The rule of thumb is that the finer the fleece, the stronger-flavored the meat.

❧ *575* ❧

Trim sheep's and goat's feet carefully, at least twice a year to help prevent foot rot.

❧ *576* ❧

Confining sheep and/or goats in a wet or muddy area on a consistent basis may also lead to foot rot. Best to fence in pastureland for grazing.

❧ *577* ❧

Pine tar is frequently used by farriers to treat split hoofs. Pine tar also combats bacterial and fungicidal infections.

❧ *578* ❧

Time to find new homes for puppies? Help puppies adjust to the separation from their mother. Tear an old sheet or rag into the same number of strips as you have puppies to sell or give away. Put the rags in the bed or box with the mother dog. When it's time to say goodbye to a puppy, send one strip of the fabric along. The puppy will have the familiar scent of his mother on the cloth to sleep close to during his first night alone.

❧ *579* ❧

Guineas sound the alarm when an intruder appears.

❧ *580* ❧

Ear mites can kill domestic rabbits. A preventative measure to take is to place 3 to 6 drops of baby oil in both ears once a month.

❧ *581* ❧

If you put a goat or horse in her stall to deliver, make sure there is no large tub of water present, to prevent a fatal delivery. It is a good idea to keep large tubs of water out of the stalls when newborn kids or foal remain in the stall with their mother until able to follow her into the pasture or until you separate them.

❧ 582 ❧

Don't fret if a newborn lamb or kid doesn't nurse imme-diately. However, if the animal appears weak, feeding its mother's colostrum ASAP may help. If a weak new-born won't nurse, milk the mother and put the colostrum into a syringe, minus the needle, of course. Squirt directly into the back of the lamb's mouth. Try to hold the animal's head up while doing so in the natural position it normally uses to nurse.

❧ 583 ❧

Chickens got wet or too cold? Newly born lamb or kid born in frigid weather? Try to save the animal by giving it a warm bath in hopes of quickly raising the body temperature.

🦋 584 🦋

To get hens to continue laying in winter, leave a light on in the chicken house.

🦋 585 🦋

When raising chicks, ducklings, or goslings, wood shavings or ground corn cobs make good bedding. Never use cedar shavings or sawdust. Due to the small size, the baby birds may eat it. Shavings from other wood varieties make ideal bedding as long as it has not been treated.

🦋 586 🦋

Are your baby chicks starting to peck each other? Make sure they're not too hot or too crowded. This can often be the cause of pecking.

❧ 587 ❧

To treat chicks that have been pecked, smear pine tar on the injured area. Continue the treatment until healing takes place.

❧ 588 ❧

Need to separate a baby chick from the others or its mother hen? Help keep it content. Put a feather duster into the box and watch the chick sleep right next to it. (The duster doesn't have to be made of real feathers either, just soft.)

❧ 589 ❧

When baby chicks arrive in the mail, dip each chick's beak into the water once as you take them out of the box and put them in their nest. This will help them locate more water and start drinking on their own.

❧ *590* ❧

To give an extra boost of energy to baby chicks, for the first two days only, add a few tablespoons of sugar to a quart of water.

❧ *591* ❧

Nursing mama dog or cat with sore, swollen tits? Clogged or infected milk ducts? Plantain poultice will help speed up the drawing-out process of the infection. The area should drain itself after this procedure. Then follow up with a fresh garlic salve, made by mixing chopped garlic and lanolin together. Apply directly to the infected region. The puppies and their mama will be grateful for your help!

❧ *592* ❧

Family farm dog attacked? Here's how to treat a dog bite wound on your animal when you can't get to a vet. Clean the wound area first. Place dog in tub. Clean wound with Epsom salt solution soaked into a clean sponge. Tie or pin around wounded area to reduce inflammation. Then prepare the following herbal treatment. Heat a pot with enough milk to make a gravy with 1 roasted onion, 2 cloves of garlic, minced and fresh or dried mullein, chopped. Select enough slices of bread to cover the wound. Use ½" thick slices of bread and spread the herb gravy on one side. Lay the bread in cheesecloth and place against wound. Wrap a large diaper or cloth around the body of the animal to cover the dressing and pin in place. Change and reapply dressings as needed, at least daily for three days. The onion draws out poisons and the garlic heals infections.

🦎 *593* 🦎

Give liquid garlic to livestock recovering from injury.

🦎 *594* 🦎

Never feed or allow your dog to eat onions. It causes anemia in canines.

🦎 *595* 🦎

Store whole eggs just like the old farmers did before refrigeration. Eggs will keep a year! Coat fresh whole eggs with a thick coating of lard. Pack into a large bucket with plenty of salt. Add more salt as you add more eggs. Affix lid and label the date of the eggs on top. Store the egg bucket in a cool place, out of the sun. The cooler the temperature, the better. A root cellar is ideal.

🦋 596 🦋

We were having trouble with a chicken eating her eggs until we put cedar shavings into the laying boxes!

🦋 597 🦋

Ever hear the country saying, you can use every part of a pig except its squeal? Well, here's proof. Don't throw out the hog's ears. It's an excellent protein snack for your dog and is veterinary approved!

❧ 598 ❧

To catch young piglets, use a butterfly net attached to a long pole or broom stick.

❧ 599 ❧

Need a domestic rabbit to mother orphans? To get a mother rabbit to nurse a kit that is not her own, rub vanilla extract on the mother rabbit's nose.

Lawn, Orchard, and Gardening

On our way to worship this morning we drove past a neighbor walking. As I watched him cross the yard I noticed not far behind him a fruit tree brimming full of ripening apples. Some had already fallen to the ground. I bet that man doesn't even pick those apples, I thought. Yet the tree continues to flourish and yield a bountiful harvest. It wasn't a huge tree, nor was it especially handsome or even majestic in appearance. Commendably, it asks for no praise before it will produce, or no special attention before reaching full maturity. The apple tree is satisfied with the necessities of life. It has no wants, requiring nothing more than is needed. And it produces in abundance, never for self or personal gain.

If only that could be said of my life. That is the way that we should all be. Doing that which we know is right, whether anyone is apparently watching or not. Are we self-motivated or does it take much encouragement from those close to us? No one cheers the apple tree on to finish the race. Go about your daily business without murmur or complaint. And certainly without a look-at-me attitude. Never perform to receive the applause of men. Work as though it was up to us to feed the five thousand while making sure that others were unaware that it was due to any effort of our own. As does the overlooked apple tree, quietly growing on the slope of a hill, yield forth much fruit in your season!

❧ 600 ☙

A large lampshade frame (minus the pleated fabric) makes a good support in the garden for small bushy plants.

❧ 601 ☙

To deter the cabbage moth (worm) from eating the leaves of your cabbage, Brussels sprouts, or kale, add 3 t. cayenne pepper to 1 quart of water. Use in a spray bottle to apply to leaves, stem, and the ground directly surrounding each plant.

❧ 602 ☙

Use straw or old hay between rows of plants to reduce the need for weeding and to retain moisture in the soil.

After harvest, turn the straw or old hay under to act as a mulch.

❀ *603* ❀

Save on garden space by growing cucumbers, water-melons, and cantaloupe beneath corn plants.

❀ *604* ❀

Another chemical-free garden spray for pest control can easily be made by adding 2 t. liquid dish detergent to warm water in a spray bottle.

❧ 605 ❧

Old-timers of bug control-cabbage plants is to lay newspaper down around the plants and heap wood ashes on top.

❧ 606 ❧

Diatomaceous earth acts as an abrasive barrier to crawling insects.

❧ 607 ❧

Reduce excess labor and save garden space by growing Irish and sweet potatoes in old car tires. The plants grow up instead of all over! Add soil to the bottom of the tire and plant seed potatoes. Add a second tire and additional top soil as the plant leaves grow tall. Water often. Manure can be added also. To harvest, remove the tires one at a time.

🦋 *608* 🦋

Plant a tall grass with your climbing peas and like vegetables to act as a natural trellis, thus eliminating the need for and labor of building a support system.

🦋 *609* 🦋

To enrich the soil in a new gardening spot, corral a horse, mule, or fence pigs in the area for several months before you start plowing and planting. The animals will remove the grass, loosen the soil, and fertilize it! And the fence will deter animals you don't want from entering the garden later.

🦋 610 🦋

To make your own high-quality potting soil, raise fishing worms in wooden boxes beneath each rabbit cage.

🦋 611 🦋

Nature's potting soil can be found in the woods by turning over an old decaying tree stump.

🦋 612 🦋

Instead of buying wooden stakes for vine plant supports, try cutting down and using green branches or bamboo.

❧ *613* ❧

Weeds are easiest to pull from the soil after a good rain.

❧ *614* ❧

Add egg shells to a quart jar of water. Use to water plants to add minerals to the soil, especially calcium.

❧ *615* ❧

Start a compost pile. To the pile add newspaper, egg shells, feathers, food scraps, dead leaves, old hay, decayed sawdust, wood ashes, hair, grass clippings, and don't forget the manure. Turn periodically.

❧ *616* ❧

Turn an old wooden ladder into a mini herb garden. Lay flat on the ground. Fill with topsoil and manure and plant a different herb in between each rung.

❧ *617* ❧

Fresh green sprouts can be raised almost anywhere without soil in days and are highly nutritious. In a wide-mouth half-gallon jar add 3 to 4 T. variety of sprout seeds. Fill ⅓ of the way with water, set up overnight. In the morning, drain off water through a screen lid or improvise. Rinse with clean water and drain again. Set at an angle to allow the seeds to drain out of direct sunlight. When the seeds show signs of growth, usually white sprouts, place near window. Continue to rinse sprouts twice daily and set at an angle to allow drainage, so the sprouts won't sour. Sprouts should be mature enough to enjoy in three to four days.

🐉 *618* 🐉

When harvesting grapes, don't forget the usefulness of the leaves. Grape leaves are often used in pickle making and as a wrapper for rice and meat for steam cooking.

🐉 *619* 🐉

Plant basil next to your tomato plants to help keep them from attack by harmful insects.

❦ 620 ❧

When using straw or old hay between your rows in the garden, wear shoes! Sometimes stickers and thorny stems get baled in the straw. Ouch!

❦ 621 ❧

Consider planting flowers and plants in the garden that you know will attract garden helpers that feed naturally on garden pests. Garden friends worth attracting are lady-bugs, praying mantis, bees, hummingbirds, house wrens, lacewing, spiders, lady beetles, and parasitic wasps.

❦ 622 ❧

Insects harmful to your garden plants are beetles, aphids (plant lice), squash bug, cabbage moth, cabbage looper, cutworm, wireworm, hornworm, pickleworm, slugs, mole crickets, grasshoppers, corn earworm, ants, squash vine borer, imported cabbageworm, white grubs, stinkbugs, and pepper weevil.

❧ 623 ❧

Birds consume lots of insects and are a natural and attractive resident of your homestead. Lure the birds to your garden area by placing a birdbath regularly filled with fresh water. This will deter them from picking a tomato for the juice. Erect a bird feeder close by. Keep filled with seeds in late autumn through early spring. Thus, the garden will be their haven when summer rolls around and they will feed on the insects at hand.

❧ 624 ❧

Make your own sticky strips for catching insects. Apply molasses thickly to a board and attach the sticky side facing down to a pole in the ground. This will draw the bugs up to the pole to the sticky trap.

❧ 625 ❧

Flour spread between rows of vegetable plants stops cabbageworms and other harmful worms and slugs. Flour actually coats the skin and kills them. (Buy it in bulk.)

❧ 626 ❧

Mineral oil or castor oil can be dripped by medicine dropper on the part of the silk of corn closest to the husk opening just as the silks begin to turn brown to control earworm. (This hand procedure would only be practical in a small family garden.)

627

Society garlic is an attractive ornamental plant, but the green stems can be chopped up and eaten like chives. It also wards off insects.

628

Garlic is an insect repellent and a healthy, nutritious herb all in one. It will also stop beetles from destroying raspberries and it protects roses as well as the rest of the garden.

629

Ants hate the herb tansy. It's great for ridding plants and the greenhouse of ants and aphids. Just steep a handful or more of tansy leaves in a quart jar and make a tea. Then strain and put in a spray bottle.

❧ 630 ❧

The leaves on the elderberry bush are poisonous, so they can be used for insect control. Add a heaping handful of crushed elderberry leaves to a quart jar and fill with boiling water. Add the lid and allow to steep. When cool, strain and apply to garden plants with a spray bottle.

❧ 631 ❧

New at gardening and looking for an easy-to-grow crop? Try planting kale seed. Kale is one of the easiest vegetables to grow, thriving well in almost any type of soil.

❧ 632 ❧

Is it time to spread lime on your garden? Spreading wood ashes (potash) gives similar results as spreading lime. Store wood ashes out of the rain in a nonflammable container until you have enough to cover the desired garden spot.

❧ 633 ❧

To spread a large quantity of wood ash (potash) on your fields, visit a local sawmill. Most wood slabs are burned on site at the sawmill. A manure spreader should do the job of spreading the ash on the desired field once you've transported it home.

※ 634 ※

Don't forget to plant some nut trees on the homestead for food. Pecan trees take seven years of growth before the first yield.

※ 635 ※

When planning your next garden consider planting some non-edible, yet highly useful items like loofa (bath sponges) and gourds for bowls, dippers, and birdhouses.

※ 636 ※

When deciding where to plant walnut trees, consider planting along a driveway. When the walnuts drop onto a driveway it makes hulling easy as the car or truck runs over and removes the large outer hull when driving on top of them. Afterwards, you collect the walnuts.

🦋 637 🦋

When planting the herb garden, it is best to grow mint in a raised bed or wooden box alone, as it tends to spread.

🦋 638 🦋

Some vegetables do taste better after a frost. Brussels sprouts and kale are good examples.

🦋 639 🦋

Radishes deter beetles when planted around crops of beans, peas, squash, melons, and cucumbers.

❧ *640* ❧

Don't harvest or trim back herbs just before a frost. Clipping causes new growth, which weakens the plants, making them susceptible to winter damage.

❧ *641* ❧

To protect your herbs from winter wind damage, plant them on the south or west side of the house.

❧ *642* ❧

Help those beautiful cut garden flowers stay fresh longer. Add 2 T. vinegar and 3 T. sugar to each quart of warm water.

❧ 643 ❧

When repotting plants, put a coffee filter in the bottom of the pot to prevent losing any soil during the watering. The filter will not obstruct natural drainage.

❧ 644 ❧

Human scent is said to deter deer and other animals from your garden. Ask your local barber to save cut hair for you. Spread it around the perimeter of the garden to ward off animal invasions.

❧ 645 ❧

Grow your own wheat grass. It's easy. In a seed starter tray, plant wheat berries just beneath the soil. (The same wheat you grind to make flour.) Water. In a few days you should see growth. When the grass has grown up, cut about an inch off the top with scissors. The grass has a slightly sweet taste to it. (Our favorite is to add clippings of wheat grass to the blender with ice and apple juice. This makes a delicious slush beverage that is also highly nutritious!) The grass will continue to grow for a week or two. Clip some each day and juice. After the grass dies, reseed and start again.

🐜 646 🐜

Want to have wheat grass or barley grass on hand year-round? When weather permits, grow a small bed of wheat grass, clip, and dry. (Dry in a gas oven or dehydrator.) Once dry, pulverize into a powder and store in jars for the winter months.

🌿 647 🌿

Be sure to purchase self-pollinating seeds if you are interested in saving seeds for future plantings.

🌿 648 🌿

To gather peas and beans for seed, plant as usual, yet do not harvest. Leave them on the vine until the pods dry. Shell and store completely dry.

🌿 649 🌿

To store seeds, place in envelopes and mark the contents. Store dry and cool. File seed envelopes in a cedar box or chest to help protect from bug infestation.

🦋 *650* 🦋

Raised beds, box planters, stepped boxes, and container gardening are ideal for those with small yard space or physical limitations. Remember, plants in containers do require more frequent watering.

🦋 *651* 🦋

Help young seedlings (transplants) get off to a good start. In early spring, place the top of a gallon milk jug with the bottom cut off over each transplant. Discard the cap. This mini housing will protect the plant from excessive wind, hot sun, or freezing temperatures. Teepees made from newspaper can be used in place of the milk jug if desired.

❧ 652 ❧

For convenient clipping of fresh culinary herbs when needed, place a window box just outside a kitchen window or install a greenhouse window.

❧ 653 ❧

Ginseng is a great medicinal cash crop. It is the most valuable herb the world has ever known. It can be found growing in the wild on shady north slopes or may be raised from seed in 90% shaded beds.

❧ 654 ❧

A ¼-acre garden of ginseng should yield an annual income exceeding $10,000! A person working full-time in other endeavors should be able to take on this size garden. A full-time ginseng grower should be able to handle a 3-acre garden with some help during weeding and picking time.

🦚 655 🦚

Orchards are best located on a northeast slope. Exposure to the morning sun dries foliage early each day during the growing season, thus reducing potential disease problems.

🦚 656 🦚

Next time there's a lightning storm in your area, be thankful! Nitrogen is released into the soil, giving a boost to the garden.

🦎 *657* 🦎

Locating an orchard on an elevated site provides shelter from spring frost.

🦎 *658* 🦎

Drape netting over berry bushes and young orchard trees to protect ripening fruit from birds.

🦎 *659* 🦎

Problems with earwigs (pincher bugs) in your garden? Roll a thick portion of newspaper into a tight cylinder and rubberband tightly. Set out in the area of infestation. The earwigs will crawl into the cylinder at night. In the morning, get up before they do and discard the paper in the trash or burn pile.

❧ 660 ❧

Want to draw beautiful butterflies to your yard or garden? Host plants and butterflies attracted by them: Butterflyweed, milkweed—monarch butterfly. Parsley, dill, fennel, and rue—black swallowtail. Passion flower—Gulf fritillary. Spicebush—spicebush swallowtail. Tulip tree—Eastern tiger swallowtail. Thistles, daisy types—American painted lady.

❧ 661 ❧

Plants that butterflies like require bright sunshine.

❧ 662 ❧

Place stones in your butterfly garden. They often light on stones and sun themselves. Basking in the sun raises their body temperature. This helps keep them active and able to fly.

🦋 663 🦋

Butterflies are attracted to flowers by color. Group flowers that butterflies like together in clusters for easy location.

🦋 664 🦋

Butterflies do not drink from open water. Create small areas of sand, earth, or mud as watering holes where you wish to draw them. Set a wet sponge in a dish with water. Rotting fruit such as bananas and apples will attract butterflies. They are drawn to moisture rather than water.

❧ 665 ❧

Hummingbirds are a beautiful and interesting addition to your yard. To ensure their presence from spring to autumn, plant a variety of plants that attract them.

❧ 666 ❧

To provide natural botanical nectar for hummingbird feed, plant a variety of the following flowers: Bee Balm, Columbine, Foxglove, Fuchsia, Lily, Petunia, Phlox, Salvia, Sweet William, Verbena, Zinnia. Shrubs and vines to plant are Azalea, Butterfly Bush, Hibiscus, Honeysuckle, Weigela, Morning Glory, Trumpet Creeper, Trumpet Honeysuckle, and Wisteria.

❧ 667 ❧

Do you enjoy the age-old craft of pressing flowers? Why not plan and plant a craft garden? Botanicals that press well are: Redbud, Crape Myrtle, Dogwood, Wisteria, Pansy, Roses, Johnny-Jump-Ups, Queen Anne's Lace, Pickerelweed, Indian Blanket, Clover, Yarrow, Ivy, Gardenia leaves, and various tree leaves.

❧ 668 ❧

Your craft garden could double as a medicinal herb garden if you include the following plants: Yarrow, Elderberry, Mint, Lemon Balm, Red Clover, Dandelion, Catnip, Purple Coneflower, and Chickweed.

❧ 669 ❧

Herbs are great to grow because they suffer little disease problems. In addition, they are hardly affected by pests and insects. The two known pests to herbs are butterfly larvae and grasshoppers. That's it!

❧ 670 ❧

There is one herb that is sure to draw raccoons, foxes, possums, and yes, the cat. Did you guess right? It's catnip.

❧ 671 ❧

Raised beds are advised for proper drainage of herb beds.

🦎 672 🦎

Parsley serves as an ideal border in a traditional four-square herb garden. The garden is equally divided into 4 sections in a + or X design. Wood or plantings (such as parsley) can be used to divide the sections.

🦎 673 🦎

Ideally, the herb garden can be planted in autumn, as it is only weather sensitive to dry winds. Snowfall creates a blanket of protection for the herbs. In fact, many herbs will continue to grow beneath the snow.

🦎 674 🦎

Cut, nip, and prune herbs regularly to stimulate continued growth. Cut chive 1" from the base of the plant.

❧ 675 ❧

See the tree how big it's grown. When it's time to take a family photo, stand the children in front of a tree you've planted or a young favorite. It is fun to see who has grown more from one year to the next. The boy or the tree.

❧ 676 ❧

Picking berries goes faster when you attach a berry-picking bucket to your belt or waist. Make your own from a plastic gallon milk or orange juice jug. Starting from the top, cut an oval opening diagonally, partially down one side, curving back up to the top. The handle can be strapped and worn at center waist. Helps keep young helpers from spilling their berries!

❧ 677 ❧

Going to work in the garden, field, or taking a hike in the hot sun? Keep a wet wash cloth in a Ziplock bag for quick cleanup or to cool your brow.

❧ 678 ❧

Here are two other ways to try to beat the heat when working outdoors: Wear a wet bandana around your neck. Place a wet wash cloth underneath your straw hat on top of your head. Rewet as needed. (A fellow we know mows the lawn with ice cubes in his pants pockets!)

❧ 679 ❧

In hot weather, reserve weeding or spending long hours in the garden for the morning or early evening hours to avoid heat exhaustion.

❧ *680* ❧

When picking wild blackberries, don't forget to wear loose clothing. Chiggers and blackberries are close companions. Chiggers like warm, bound places. Take along a pair of small snips to clip a clear path through the thorny bushes as you pick.

❧ *681* ❧

Want the easiest berry to harvest? Try the blueberry. They grow at a height that eliminates the need for bending and they're thornless. (There are cultivated varieties of thornless blackberry bushes available too.)

❧ *682* ❧

What can you plant that insects absolutely will not bother? Onions and garlic. If you are having trouble with insects eating anything in the garden, plant some onion and/or garlic around or between other plants.

❧ 683 ❧

Try mixing crushed garlic and water together for an effective insect-control garden spray.

❧ 684 ❧

Keep borers from drilling into the base of fruit trees in the orchard by planting a circle of onions or garlic around the trunk.

❧ 685 ❧

Garlic requires a full 12 months in the ground to yield a nice-size bulb. Be patient in harvesting. It will not be hampered by cold temperatures, snow, or frost.

❧ 686 ❧

Natural Ant Mound Eradicator. Pick and dry pyrethrum flowers (type of chrysanthemum). Add 1 t. dried, ground pyrethrum to 2 gallons of water and add ¼ c. liquid soap. Shake well and pour one cup on each mound. Repeat treatment one hour later to thoroughly penetrate and saturate the tunnels.

❧ 687 ❧

Rock salt is an old-fashioned weed killer and quite economical too. Sprinkle it on cracks in walkways or wherever unwanted weeds grow. Beware! Rock salt makes the ground sterile. Keep away from your vegetable garden or plush lawn.

❧ 688 ❧

The easiest and surest way to grow herbs is to locate and allow them to grow naturally, in the wild. Using a copy of your land survey as a guide, draw a map of your land. As you locate herbs growing, write the names of the herbs on the map in the existing location. Harvest as needed, but always be sure to leave some behind for future availability.

❧ 689 ☙

Save tea and coffee grounds to apply to the base of acid-loving plants such as the azalea.

❧ 690 ☙

Peaches ripen quickly if placed in a box covered with newspaper.

In the Tool Shed and the Great Outdoors

Affordable waterfront property can be yours with just a spade or shovel, wheelbarrow, bucket, plenty of water, and cement. That's right, a backyard lily pond. We built one while living in the suburbs, desiring a taste of nature, while waiting for our move to the country. This is a project sure to delight young and old alike. When others hear you've got tadpoles, look out! You'll find yourself carrying jars of the little critters into the most unsuspecting places. We've been spotted at the local church house on midweek meeting with a few jars ourselves.

Several times a year the frogs invaded our little backyard pond. In the evenings during a "courting" session, if you closed your eyes, you would think that you fell asleep and woke up in the midst of the Okefenokee swamp! Most neighbors are disturbed by a barking dog at night. While our contribution to the midnight concerto was frogs! I kid you not! Fortunately our neighbors liked the sounds of the swamp as much as we did. Sometimes it actually was a little overdone.

Once, after a few hard rains, water stood beneath our house and the frogs made their way up under our bedroom floor! This serenade was a little too close for comfort. I felt like they were taking over the place on this occasion.

Each morning, before the sun got too hot, you could observe the frogs and see the long strands of pearl-size black eggs they laid. On one such occasion, I counted a dozen "courting pairs," then noticed that one frog appeared to be alone. All of a sudden the bachelor frog leaped right on the head of another frog, attempting to separate a mating pair. When that attempt failed, it leaped again onto another couple. What a humorous sight! When I described our observations to my mother, she said she'd seen the same incident on National Geographic! Who needs T.V. when you have your own backyard wildlife? And it doesn't require any grant money to study. The specimens willingly appear without a formal request. Although we do miss the swamp sounds of the night, their presence has been pleasantly replaced by a chorus of bobwhites, crickets, an owl, rooster, wild turkeys, and even coyotes as we contemplate sleep on a summer's night.

691

Don't stack firewood too close to the house to avoid termite infestation.

692

Keep all wood used on the exterior of the house, barn, and railings, etc. either painted or stained. Termites attack raw or untreated wood.

693

Leaving the bark on the wood used for porch and deck railings has a rustic appeal to it. However, just under the bark is where bugs like to make their home. You will have to replace this wood much sooner, if you leave the bark on the wood.

❧ 694 ❧

Want to build on the waterfront? Don't build too close to a creek or spring branch where trees are standing. When a rainstorm or tornado comes, trees near the water's edge are the first to fall.

❧ 695 ❧

If caught outdoors during a tornado, find a dry ditch to crawl into. Select one without a lot of trees nearby, if possible.

❧ 696 ❧

Want the house close to a pond? Keep in mind that mosquitoes breed in stagnant water. Choose spring branch or creek sites where there is a constant moving of the water over pond sites when building.

697

Is the house hot in summer? Here are a few things you can do outside to help. If you live in a mobile home, paint white roofing coating on the roof. This will lessen the heat that penetrates through the top. Build a covered porch onto the portion of the house that gets the most direct sun. Plant a shade tree to block direct summer sun's rays from the house. Check with a local nursery for tree species that grow fast in your area.

698

Need to winterize your home and outbuildings? Not enough time? Stack square bales of old hay or straw around the outer perimeter of your buildings to block cold air from coming up under the foundation.

❦ *699* ❦

The best time to shop for a new house or property is right after a heavy rain. It's a good time to spot potential problems.

❦ *700* ❦

Want to build your own porch and lawn furniture? Woods that will hold up well to outdoor weather are cypress, cedar, and teak.

❦ *701* ❦

Quilted vests are an ideal layer of winter clothing when performing physical labor outdoors. Arms remain free to work unrestrained.

❧ *702* ❧

Spend most of your time outdoors? A man's beard naturally provides warmth in winter and protection from the sun's penetrating rays in summer!

❧ *703* ❧

Cool, loose-fitting clothes of natural fibers such as 100% cotton or linen are best to wear when working outdoors in the summer heat.

❧ *704* ❧

When working outside in the chill of winter, layer for warmth. In the morning and evening you will need the most on. Wear quilted coveralls. As the sun warms, remove a layer. Ladies in dresses can be warm outdoors too by wearing a layer of tights, wool socks, leggings and/or sweatpants or flannel bloomers. (If the pioneer women trekked across the nation in dresses, we can get along in them too!)

🦢 705 🦢

When selecting a site for an outhouse stay far enough away from spring branches and creeks to avoid polluting the waterways. Many plain families have been forced to put in septic tanks because of this oversight.

🦢 706 🦢

Fishing Tip. The local barbershop has served as an information source long before satellite dishes and microwave communications were common place. Lowell picked this little pearl up from a local fisherman in the barbershop during a recent haircut: "No point in going fishin' until the dogwoods bloom and the east wind quits blowing 'cause the fish won't bite."

❧ *707* ❧

When serving meals outside in the spring and summer, for fly control, place a fan near the food table. Flies will not light in windy areas.

❧ *708* ❧

Citronella wards off mosquitoes. Use citronella candles or the citronella plant itself in outdoor social spaces such as the porch.

❧ *709* ❧

Termites and rot attack unpainted, unstained wood quickly. If the natural look is preferred, don't forget to use a clear wood sealer on your wood house, deck, porches, railings, etc.

❧ *710* ❧

Need to put up a building in a hurry, and inexpensively? If you don't have cedar logs on your property, purchase them locally and have them sawn yourself. You'll save about ⅓ of the cost of purchasing lumber from the big chain lumber stores and you don't have to wait for cedar lumber to dry. Cedar can be sawn and ready to use for building as soon as you need it!

❧ *711* ❧

Save empty plastic pancake syrup bottles (and other squirt top containers) for compact water jugs to take along outdoors. Place inside your jacket in winter to keep from freezing. In hot weather, fill the bottle ¾ full and place in the freezer until solid. Once you have the bottle outdoors, the ice will slowly melt, providing you with a cool drink of water for hours. Great to take along when working in the garden or on any strenuous outdoor project.

❧ *712* ❧

Keep the outhouse smelling fresh. Sprinkle lime after each use. Also, supply the outhouse with a box of baby wipes when no water is available for washing the hands.

❧ *713* ❧

If you have a catalpa tree growing at your place, you've got live fishing bait. Each summer worms that catfish just love hatch on the tree!

❧ *714* ❧

Rooster livers make great bait for catching catfish. Rooster liver is tougher than chicken liver, thus staying on the hook better!

❧ *715* ❧

A sure way to lure crabs every time is to place raw chicken parts into a crab trap and lower into the water.

❧ *716* ❧

Keep your tools from rusting. Place a piece of charcoal or a sachet of kitty litter in the tool box to absorb the moisture.

❧ *717* ❧

Make it easier to drive screws into hard wood by greasing the screws with soap first.

❧ *718* ☙

Applying soap or linseed oil to nails reduces the chances of wood splitting and lessens pounding. It saves work!

❧ *719* ☙

Wonder how to prevent the head of your hammer from getting loose? Wooden handles sometimes shrink as they dry out. Tighten the loose head, then stand the hammer head in a container of linseed oil.

❧ *720* ☙

Make a burn barrel for your paper trash by cutting out one end of a 55-gallon drum. Then drill a few holes in the side for air circulation. Set up on top of a few rocks or concrete blocks to keep the inside dry and to prevent the barrel from rusting. A great way to keep a contained fire where permissible.

❧ 721 ❧

A non-working chest freezer with a good rubber seal makes a good root cellar. Simply bury it in the ground up to the hinges. If the insides of the freezer start to sweat, open the lid on a day when the temperature is 30° F or below. Leave open until the contents and chest have had a chance to chill.

❧ 722 ❧

Like to have a root cellar, but there's no basement? That's right! It's not as difficult as it sounds. You'll have to have a little bulldozer work done first and you'll need to purchase an old bus too. Remove soil, drive the bus into place. Cover it with dirt so that only the rear doors are exposed. Construct a wooden frame and walkway to keep the soil from falling in the entrance area and a door to conceal the rear of the bus. Makes a handy storm shelter too!

723

On your way to a picnic? Need to keep a casserole hot? Here's an easy way to keep things warm. Heat 2 bricks in an oven. Once hot, wrap them in a towel and set in the bottom of an ice chest. Place the hot dish on top of the bricks. Cover with another towel or small blanket. Keep the chest shut until ready to eat.

724

Another way to serve a hot meal on a picnic without re-heating is to prepare your dinner in a pressure cooker. Don't remove the lid until time to eat. The food in the cooker should stay hot for a couple of hours. Wrap in towels and transport in an ice chest, if desired.

☙ 725 ☙

If you pour your own concrete pond, do not immediately fill with fish or plants. The water will be toxic to fish and plants for several days. A pond or water garden is habitable for fish and plants once you notice algae growth on the sides and the water turns brackish yet transparent.

☙ 726 ☙

Mosquitoes cannot survive in water unless it is stagnant. Incorporate a water fountain or pump into your backyard pond.

❧ *727* ❧

A small pump to help oxygenate the water is necessary in order for fish to survive in a homemade pond or water garden.

❧ *728* ❧

Enjoy a backyard pond but not the mosquitoes? To eliminate mosquito larvae from a small water garden or pond in your yard, pour a biodegradable coating of oil (such as vegetable oil) across the top of the water.

❧ *729* ❧

An empty grapefruit sack with drawstring can be filled with dishes or other supplies when camping and hung from the end of a tree branch to keep the critters out.

❧ 730 ❧

Like working outdoors, but not the dirty fingernails afterwards? Dig you fingernails into a bar of soap and lather your hands without rinsing off the soap just before going outdoors. After a hard day's work outside, your hands will wash up nicely and your nails will too!

❧ 731 ❧

Need a funnel you can discard after one use? Cut the top half off of a plastic gallon milk jug and turn upside down. It even has a handle!

❧ 732 ❧

Use the bottom half of plastic milk jugs to sort and store nails, screws, tacks, washers, etc. in the tool shed.

❧ *733* ❧

Need to take down a dead tree or two? If the tree overlooks a nice view, fashion it with a chainsaw into a rustic chair, leaving a base and a backrest. It will resemble the upping posts that were historically used by early Americans to mount riding horses. (Our three dead trees transformed nicely into two chairs and a table.)

❧ *734* ❧

Need to paint a metal object yet keep a portion of it unpainted, such as a metal ruler mounted to a metal case? Oil or grease the portion you do not want to receive paint. A grease gun comes in handy for this purpose. Spray paint and allow to dry. Wipe the paint residue right off the coated area with a rag without disturbing the painted portion of the metal!

❧ 735 ❧

Pick up or have a load of sand delivered to create an instant play area for the children. (A plastic wading pool makes a great instant sandbox container.) Place under a shade tree or construct a tarp canopy overhead to keep the children from becoming sunburned in summer.

❧ 736 ❧

Going on a summer hike in the woods? Strap a dog tick and flea collar around each ankle for protection.

❧ 737 ❧

Remove and use the drum from an old washing machine to contain a camp fire.

Index